DATE DUE

M

He isn't an undream of anaesthetized impersons,or a cosmic

comfortstation,or a transcendentally sterilized lookiesoundie-

feelietastiesmellie. He is a healthily complex,a naturally ho-

mogeneous,citizen of immortality. The now of his each pity-

ing free imperfect gesture,his any birth or breathing,insults

perfected inframortally millenniums of slavishness. He is a

little more than everything,he is democracy;he is alive:he is

ourselves.

—E. E. Cummings, Introduction to

Collected Poems, 1938

e.e. cummings

the art
of his
poetry

BY NORMAN FRIEDMAN

BALTIMORE: THE JOHNS HOPKINS PRESS

Second Printing, 1962

Distributed in Great Britain by Oxford University, London

Printed in the United States of America

Library of Congress Catalog Card Number 60-9771

This book has been brought to publication with the
assistance of a grant from The Ford Foundation.

PREFACE

All the references in the text, with the exception of those in the Postscript, are to poem numbers and page numbers of the complete collected edition, *Poems: 1923–1954* (New York, Harcourt, Brace and Co., 1954). The dating of many of the poems appearing in the first three volumes of this collection, however, is misleading. The archetype edition of *Tulips and Chimneys,* dated 1922, was published in 1937: collation reveals that less than half of the poems in the original manuscript appeared under that title in 1923, the remainder having constituted more than half of *&* and all of *XLI Poems,* both of which were published in 1925. I have therefore reassembled all of the poems of the original *Tulips and Chimneys* under that title and have dated them 1922.

I owe much to many people who assisted me in one way or another as I wrote this book, but most to E. E. Cummings and his wife, Marion Morehouse, who have been more than generous in their willingness over a period of many years to talk with me, answer my letters, and send me materials that I could not otherwise have obtained. My wife, to whom this book is dedicated, read and corrected the manuscript several times, and also helped me in other and more important ways. Charles A. McLaughlin, a friend and colleague, read it all as I wrote it and discussed it with me for hours at a time. For Stanley Edgar Hyman's helping hand, I am everlastingly grateful. Grateful thanks are also due to Mrs. Ebba Hammerberg for typing the manuscript.

I want further to thank my fellow Cummingsites, Rudolph Von Abele, Robert Lawrence Beloof, David Burns, George J. Firmage, Charles Norman, and Robert E. Wegner, for their letters and for sending me their various published and unpublished works. And I am indebted to the Modern Language Association for awarding me a small grant-in-aid to purchase books and microfilms.

Permission to quote Mr. Cummings' poetry has been granted by the poet and by Harcourt, Brace & Co. Henry Holt & Co. and Jonathan Cape, Ltd. have granted the permission to quote from Robert Frost's poem, "Choose Something Like a Star."

Part of Chapter One appeared in *The Literary Review,* and Chapter Three appeared, in a slightly different form, in *Publications of the Modern Language Association.* The kindness of the editors of these journals in allowing me to use this material is appreciated.

For further information about Cummings' publications and critics, the reader may consult Paul Lauter's mimeographed work, *E. E. Cummings: Index to First Lines and Bibliography of Works by and about the Poet* (Denver: Alan Swallow, 1955), and George J. Firmage, *E. E. Cummings: A Bibliography* (Middletown, Conn.: Wesleyan University Press, 1960).

October 1959
The University of Connecticut   *Norman Friedman*

CONTENTS

"Works of art are of an infinite loneliness and with nothing to be so little reached as with criticism. Only love can grasp and hold and fairly judge them" [Rilke]. In my proud and humble opinion, those two sentences are worth all the soi-disant criticism of the arts which has ever existed or will ever exist.

—E. E. Cummings, *i: six nonlectures*

INTRODUCTION criticism

Every age is an age of transition, but today in poetry we are witnessing an especially poignant transition: the giants of modern poetry, those who gave it its unique character and who by now are being taught in the classroom as if their works were already classics, are nearing the end of their careers. Pound, Eliot, Stevens, Frost, Williams, Cummings —they are still, with the exception of Stevens, alive among us (in 1959) and producing important work. But they are in their sixties, seventies, and eighties. Already it seems to many of us that our middle-aged poets

—Auden, Spender, Roethke, Shapiro, Lowell, and others—were only yesterday our younger poets. And with some surprise we realize that our really younger poets—such as Wilbur, Coxe, Hall, and Wright— have established firm positions and are themselves not only teaching but also being taught in the classroom. What makes this transition especially poignant is not simply the inevitable sequence of generations; it is more significantly that there is such a difference, for better or for worse, between the older and the younger poets. This difference—and it is a big one—is basically the result of our new poets' not having to go it alone. Today, the rising poet is not only likely to have an academic post, he is also an heir of the modern mode which has by now become his tradition. We are witnessing the passing of our great generation of innovators and experimentalists.

Cummings undoubtedly has a high place among them. He has never been without a strong reputation, and in the last decade alone he has been showered with honors. In 1950 he received the Fellowship of the Academy of American Poets; in 1952–1953 he was appointed to the Charles Eliot Norton Professorship at Harvard; in 1954 a complete collected edition of his poetry was published; in 1955 he received a special citation for that collection from the National Book Awards; in 1957 he won the Boston Fine Arts Festival Poetry Award; and in that same year he was awarded the Bollingen Prize in Poetry. The year 1958 was an *annus mirabilis,* witnessing the publication of no fewer than six Cummings volumes: a translation of a selection of his poems into German; another into Italian; a reprint of *Eimi* in paperback form; a collection of his fugitive prose pieces; a biography; and a new book of poems. And I understand that there are in preparation a full-length bibliography and a collection of essays on his work by various hands. Further, Cummings is in constant demand for poetry readings, and invariably attracts large and enthusiastic audiences.

I / It is clear, then, that Cummings has earned a stature that calls for a full-scale assessment of his poetry as a whole. Yet it is curious that he has less frequently had the sort of concentrated critical attention that his noted contemporaries have had. There are books on Eliot, Pound, Auden, Stevens, Frost, Thomas, Williams, Jeffers, and others, but none —except Charles Norman's recent biography—on Cummings. It is true that many well-known writers—Pound, Dos Passos, Williams, Frankenberg, Graves, Marianne Moore, Spencer, Auden, W. T. Scott, J. P. Bishop, Gregory and Zaturenska, for example—have always thought very highly of him; and it is true that many younger critics—S. V. Baum, George Haines IV, Rudolph Von Abele, David Burns, for example—have written of his work with perception and enthusiasm. The fact remains, however, that many of our most influential critics— Blackmur, Ransom, Wilson, Honig, Jarrell, Untermeyer, Matthiessen, G. S. Fraser, Kazin, and Bogan—have not known quite what to make of him.

There are several reasons for this division in appreciation, and chief among them, I believe, is that some of our reigning critics are bound by certain limiting conceptions as to what poetry should be and that these conceptions do not happen to apply very comfortably to Cummings. To look in his work for the signs of a tragic vision, for an ambivalence of structure, for a studied use of verbal ambiguity, for the display of a metaphysical wit, for the employment of mythic fragments, for the climax of a spiritual conversion—this is to look for things which are simply not there. And to complain, accordingly, that he lacks maturity of vision, variety of forms, intelligibility of diction, true seriousness, a sense of artistic purpose, and development is to misconstrue the nature both of critical principles and of Cummings' poetry. To assume, on the one hand, that such conceptions cover the entire range of excellence in lyric poetry is to rule out—as has already happened in the case of some of the most famed poets in the history of English literature—much that is of genuine value when seen in the light of other principles; while to apply, on the other hand, such conceptions to poetry which they do not fit is to distort the true nature of that poetry. This has happened to Cummings. Paradoxically, however, many of the critics who have been unable intellectually to assent to his work have nevertheless confessed to a certain furtive delight which it brings them. Although they like the poetry, that is, they have difficulty in taking it seriously.

It is the purpose of this book, then, to attempt a more complete and accurate definition of just what it is that Cummings can do, and on that basis to suggest how his very real accomplishment may be viewed in a more adequate light. I hope to do so in terms of a criticism that will bridge the gap between heart and head—a gap found in so many of his interpreters. To feel delight and yet to be persuaded of the insignificance of its causes is not the proper state of mind in which to approach the poetry of Cummings—or of any other poet. Indeed, it is the right of any poet to be evaluated in terms of what he does rather than in terms of what he should do, and it is the duty of his critic to allow the work to flower before him in terms of its own inner necessities rather than in those of his own favored prescriptions. I suppose that there are standards external to the poet against which he is ultimately to be judged, but surely the critic must be careful that these standards are capable of including the wide variety of things that we may cherish rather than merely what a given fashion has taught us to care for.

If Cummings does not have a tragic vision, he does have another type of vision, which is sufficiently serious to serve as the basis of a significant lyric poetry—if not of tragic drama or fiction—and it should be judged accordingly. Similarly, if it be granted that poetry has other ends than the embodiment of symbolic tensions, then the variety of Cummings' forms will appear; if it be realized that a poet can and usually does impose a form upon the language he uses, then it will be seen that his language is not unintelligible; if it be admitted that technical devices can have other uses than that of reconciling opposites, then it will be clear that his experiments do serve legitimate artistic ends; if his more than forty years of dedication to his art be considered, then the claim that Cummings is a haphazard workman will be confounded; and if his poetry be read attentively from beginning to end, then it will be obvious that it does reveal a steady development toward maturity.

II / In order to define the nature of Cummings' poetry, and consequently to suggest how it may be evaluated, I shall search out its sources in his view of life, analyze its varieties, and inquire into its methods. Thus I intend to trace the *why* of his work, then the *what,* and finally the *how.*

An inquiry such as this into a group of poems by a given author begins with the mind of the poet. For it takes a man with certain qualities of imagination and sensibility to write not only poems (rather than something else) but poems of certain kinds. What he does and how he does it, that is, are given shape by the force and direction of his inner necessities; what he can conceive of determines what and how he will write, or not write. By this I do not mean that we shall be concerned with the poet's biography or philosophy or psychology, but simply with such qualities of his artistic imagination and sensibility as may be inferred from the character of the person he has invented to speak his poems, the attitudes and ideas he has attributed to him, and the kinds of subjects he has chosen to elicit a response in that speaker. Accordingly, in the first chapter, I try to focus the entire study in terms of Cummings' own values.

It is the response of the speaker, whether dramatic or rhetorical, to the various sorts of situations in which Cummings has placed him, that defines the shape of the poem, and since his response is determined by his character, thought, and the various subjects which compel his attention, it follows in Chapter Two that I endeavor to outline the nature and variety of the different kinds of poems Cummings writes as a result of his having a certain sort of vision.

In Chapter Three, I attempt to analyze the various languages with which this speaker is endowed in order to express these responses, and to evaluate the use of these languages as appropriate to and consistent with his nature and temperament, and the situations in which he finds himself. Similarly, in Chapter Four, I seek to analyze the special techniques used in connection with the speaker's languages, and to evaluate their use as vivifying and intensifying devices.

In Chapter Five, as a demonstration in a particular case of all that has gone before as well as of the workings of Cummings' constructive powers, I trace the growth, through its manuscript variants, of a recent poem.

In the Conclusion I discuss separately the question of Cummings' development; and finally, in the Postscript, I review his latest volume, *95 Poems*.

I have my own stern claims and perfect circle. It denies the name of duty to many offices that are called duties. But if I can discharge its debts, it enables me to dispense with the popular code. If any one imagines that this law is lax, let him keep its commandment one day.

And truly it demands something godlike in him who has cast off the common motives of humanity, and has ventured to trust himself for a taskmaster. High be his heart, faithful his will, clear his sight, that he may in good earnest be doctrine, society, law, to himself, that a simple purpose may be to him as strong as iron necessity is to others!

—Emerson, *Self-Reliance*

CHAPTER ONE # vision

We must begin our inquiry into the nature of Cummings' poetic art with the character of his speaker, his attitudes and ideas, and the subjects that compel his attention. For it is from these that we may infer the scope and quality of the poet's artistic imagination and sensibility.

I / The poet as a man like other men is always more than the poet as artist, for the artist must select those aspects of the man that will make viable poems. If Cummings has personally experienced hunger, as the preface to the Modern Library edition of *The Enormous Room* implies, the speaker of his poems has no interest in the problem whatsoever—except to scorn it. It would be fruitful, as one way of defining the character of the speaker, to seek out the nature of this relationship between artist and man, using only the most general and commonly known biographical facts, in order to see not only what has been put into but also what has been left out of the poems.

Now with regard to this significant relationship between artist and man, there are, it seems to me, three distinct possibilities: (1) the speaker of the poems, or persona, may be integrated with the workaday personality and pursuits of its author, as with Frost's speaker, for example, who is a New England farmer even as Frost himself was at one time; (2) the author may deliberately create a poetic persona and then transform himself in its image, organizing his personal life and concerns to conform to that pattern, as did Whitman, for example, who consciously adopted the dress, manner, and pursuits of the bard who spoke his poems; or (3) author and speaker may be completely dissociated, as, for example, is the case with Wallace Stevens, who as a man was an insurance executive, while the speaker of his poems is a subtle and imaginative metaphysician.

In other words, the persona of an author's poems may be a normal man with normal concerns, even as its author is; or it may be a man apart from men, as its author has become; or it may be a man apart from men, even while its author—who may be a pediatrician, a businessman, a critic, or an editor, for example—is involved in the business of the everyday world. And perhaps because our society has not had, at least until the recent opening of the academic gates to artists, a recognized socio-economic role for the poet as such to fill, we might say that the third or dissociative relationship is the most typical (for what poet can support himself and a family by his writing?); that the first or integrative relationship is the most rare (for how many vocational activities can today be turned to poetic uses?—farming is ideal but full of practical obstacles); and that the second or transformative relationship is the most difficult to achieve (for which of our poets has either money enough or sufficient endurance in its absence simply to live as he wishes?).

It should be obvious enough by now that the relationship between Cummings and his speaker is of the second kind, and it has been made possible by endurance—or better still, integrity—rather than by a private income. His speaker is never involved in the world of work and routine which takes up the largest part of the lives of most men. In contrast to Frost's persona, he has no wood to cut, no apples to pick, and no promises to keep; he watches out of a window, walks the streets at night, travels, sits on a hill overlooking a view or in a saloon listening to the click of billiard balls. He is a detached observer and commentator rather than a participant; he is always either alone or with his lady; he never has a time clock to punch, a train to catch, a bill to pay, or a baby to feed. Or, as William James has described the type:

> Only your mystic, your dreamer, or your insolvent tramp or loafer, can afford so sympathetic an occupation, an occupation which will change the usual standards of human value in the twinkling of an eye, giving to foolishness a place ahead of power, and laying low in a minute the distinctions which it takes a hard-working conventional man a lifetime to build up. You may be a prophet, at this rate; but you cannot be a worldly success.
>
> —*On a Certain Blindness in Human Beings*

Although such a character closely resembles its author in many respects, no regrets for such detachment are ever mentioned in the poems. As opposed, say, to such an image of the modern artist as Joyce has created in Stephen Daedalus, whatever hunger, doubt, or even despair we imagine Cummings must have endured as a consequence of such a view, his speaker is completely free of them, busy as he is with songs of joy. And this is the incredible thing about Cummings' poetry—how completely the man has been transformed into the artist, for his mode of life has involved absolutely no compromise between the character of the speaker he has created and the demands of everyday existence. It is just possible, indeed, that Cummings himself fully believes and acts exactly as his speaker believes and acts.

The speaker of Cummings' poems, then, is always a poet and a painter, and this has been a matter of endurance almost ritualistic in its disciplined and consistently sustained self-abnegation: the man has in effect died that the artist might live. For if the artist enjoys a certain amount of freedom from drudgery and nagging routine of which we of the "really unreal" world might feel somewhat envious, he also in exchange denies himself the solace of family and physical security which most of us would be reluctant indeed to surrender. And even more "dangerously" (a favorite word of his) he has taken, by a deliberate effort of will, his destiny altogether into his own hands, so that whatever becomes of him, he is entirely responsible. It has been, for him, an exchange of one kind of responsibility for another, and this voluntary assumption of freedom is a conclusive sign, if a sign is needed, of his absolute moral seriousness.

He ran a great risk and he has won. Living penuriously for many years, and always oblivious to the ebb and flow of literary fashion, Cummings has weathered war and peace, depression and prosperity, old critics and new critics, aesthetes and Marxists, and he has remained himself—a force to be reckoned with in any consideration of modern poetry. The ritual of surrender has brought him out on the other side. The artist who swallows the man becomes in turn a man again—only this time a man who has been purged, cleansed, and purified. The poet, for Cummings, is merely the type of the true man, and all true men are poets: men who can see with clear eyes, feel with unconditioned emotions, and love without fear; men who are whole, entire, and alive.

If this describes the *what* of his speaker's character, we have next to inquire into the *why*. Thus, if he dwells apart, as we have seen, and observes, reflects, and feels, he does so as the servant of one cause only —freshness of response and accuracy in its expression:

O Distinct
Lady of my unkempt adoration
if i have made
a fragile certain

song under the window of your soul
it is not like any songs   (VII: 37)

Love, however hackneyed a source for other poets, is for this speaker a
positive inspiration for freshness and accuracy. His attitude toward his
lady is courtly and reverential. Thus devoted, he recognizes the ultimate irony of his attempt, because the true response can never be
captured in language:

yours is the music for no instrument

.   .   .   .

yours are the poems i do not write.   (III: 65–66)

Similarly, the speaker, being a man, cannot feel so directly as his lady:

—the best gesture of my brain is less than
your eyelids' flutter . . .   (VII: 209)

And yet, he is "the poet who is afraid/ only to mistranslate/ a rhythm
in your hair" (VIII: 209), and asks her not to wonder if he happens to
"make a millionth poem which will not wholly/ miss you" (IV: 75).

Conversely, the chief obstacle to the true response is submitting to
mass life, accepting the second-hand and the third-rate, conditioning
one's feelings to conform with the will of the mob. With regard to
society at large he pictures himself as the Greenwich Village and Pari-
sian Bohemian artist, living in a garret, eating aspirin, and coughing
too much (XVI: 176–77). He is an amused and angry spectator of the
world in general—which is peopled by celebrities, famous fatheads,
salesmen, and big shots, and ruled by the hairless old—and sympa-
thetically identifies himself with minorities, the outcast, the under-

privileged, liking (as Joe Gould does) Negroes, Indians, and bums (27: 294-95):

> poets yeggs and thirsties

> since we are spanked and put to sleep by dolls . . .

> .   .   .   .   .

>   . . . let us investigate
> thoroughly each one his optima rerum first   (XXXI: 186-87)

As the world goes, he and such like are "anyones" and "noones" as opposed to the important "someones" and "everyones"; tramps with no future, touching their crumpled caps and smoking found butts (VI: 226-27; cf. 4: 431). And is this only romantic Bohemianism? Have not prophets walked among the lowly of the earth and consorted with criminals as a sign of their humility?

As a poet he thus retains the purity of his vision apart from the compulsions and shams of society, apart from what people expect him to be:

> (nor has a syllable of the heart's eager dim
> enormous language loss or gain from blame or praise)   (LXIII: 268)

And as a man he thereby achieves selfhood, which, as we have seen, is the goal directing his cause: to be self-reliant in Emerson's sense; to be free from dependence upon external goods in the Stoic sense; to become fully conscious of oneself in the Epicurean sense; a man, in short, who

> (would rather make than have and give than lend
> —being through failures born who cannot fail

> having no wealth but love,who shall not spend
> my fortune(although endlessness should end)   (11: 285)

This is a man who knows death but chooses life, who knows grief but chooses joy, who knows fear but chooses love; one who, in imitation of Christ (whom a Unitarian Cummings reveres with a personal devotion—50: 455), redeems chaos by remaining true (31: 296-97). This is a man in harmony with nature, not demanding a deathless life on earth (19: 290–91), "his autumn's winter being summer's spring" (37: 300). He is unafraid of the coming of winter and death because of his confidence in the ultimate return of spring and life (27: 443–44).

It is no wonder, therefore, that he makes war (56: 315–17) on "all/ unfools of unbeing" who "set traps for his heart,/ lay snares for his feet" (55: 315), for the portion of the true poet-man in our society is not a sweet one. He is an eccentric person cultivating his eccentricity, a "crazy man" upon whom frightened and respectable "mrs and mr" pull down their shades (15: 360), a threat of failure in a world of success, a living reproach upon whom it spits. But he is a "fool and man" in whose image the speaker chooses to live (56: 315–17) because he is a useless failure (19: 343–44); a "wise fool" who is a thief because "someone called they" have caught him stealing apples in someone's "private" orchard (III: 390); a "fiend" and "angel," "coward, clown, traitor, idiot, dreamer, beast"—

such was a poet and shall be and is

—who'll solve the depths of horror to defend
a sunbeam's architecture with his life:
and carve immortal jungles of despair
to hold a mountain's heartbeat in his hand   (XXII: 402)

This is the mask through which Cummings speaks. Cutting Gordian knots with the keen edge of a rhyme, his speaker sees this world as cleanly divided between good and evil, right and wrong, and, in so doing, simply rises above the whole struggle into a transcendent world which is one, and full of love.

II / The moral and emotional values that this speaker entertains as a consequence of having such a character derive basically from this position of transcendence which he assumes.

Perhaps the key to the thought of Cummings' persona is to be found in the fact that, in his universe, there is evil but no sin. It is as if we were all still living in an Eden in which no command has yet been given, and all, except the speaker and a few others like him, are afraid of eating of its fruits. If it were not for this fear, we could, if we would, still reach out and eat of all the fruits of the garden, for we have never lost it nor has God ever cursed us: "the thing perhaps is/ to eat flowers and not to be afraid" (XXXIII: 190). Man, for him, is still noble, virtuous, and not just *potentially* in a state of Grace. This is a prelapsarian morality, a vision of life without the happy fault, a philosophy of extreme self-determinism and free will. It is perhaps the Unitarianism of Cummings' childhood; it is perhaps how a sensitive child looks at life.

In depicting his speaker in such an untheological stance, Cummings is, as in so many other respects, outside what appears to be the dominant literary fashion. An interesting contrast is also provided, for example, by Wordsworth's "The World Is Too Much with Us" and Housman's "The Laws of God, The Laws of Man," both of which are in other respects instances of the romantic tradition in which Cummings writes. In the first poem, the speaker, depressed by the spiritual deadness of his world, longs fruitlessly for citizenship in an earlier time; in the second poem, the speaker, frustrated by the discordance he feels between religious and secular demands and his own impulses, and restrained by the fact that he "cannot fly/ To Saturn nor to Mercury," decides he must yield to law and deny his own impulses. The difference is that with Cummings no such unfulfilled longing or deadlocked frustration hampers the speaker. In a situation similar to those confronting Wordsworth's and Housman's speakers, he concludes characteristically, "listen:there's a hell/ of a good universe next door; let's go" (XIV: 397). Man's mortality is, for him, no necessary hindrance; man's capacity for making mistakes is not built into the universe; Cummings' hell is not real to him in the way that Dante's was; and the only necessity that he acknowledges is the movement toward joy.

His reaction to suffering and evil is, since they are wholly manmade, hate unalloyed with pity; he has no sense at all of man's helplessness

due to historical or metaphysical causes. And his reaction to courage
and love is, since they are wholly divine, admiration unspoiled by second thoughts; he has no idea whatever of man's fundamental am-
bivalences due to environmental and psychological causes. He who is
truly alive is truly self-reliant and self-created; he is beyond the reach
of external causation; his life is entirely within; and he has reached
that state of beatitude described by John Donne as characteristic of the
soul after the Resurrection: ". . . she reads without spelling, and knows
without thinking, and concludes without arguing; she is at the end of
her race, without running; in her triumph without fighting. . . . She
knows truly, and easily, and immediately, and everlastingly" (Sermon
XIX). And the essential point is, for Cummings, that we may achieve
this status on earth and without heavenly intervention.

This sense of detachment also partially explains the unusual virulence
of his satire, for if we are ourselves wholly responsible for whatever
foolishness we are guilty of and whatever betrayals we commit, then
it follows that the satirist can bite and snarl, laugh and rage, fume and
storm in his effort to get us to change our ways, and be without pity
for those who refuse to listen. It helps to explain the rare tenderness of
his love poetry as well, for the lover is not affrighted by the skull beneath the skin when he kisses his lady, nor is he dismayed by the tug
of guilt as he embraces her.

For those who do listen, the world is transformed; the true man and
woman transcend the "real" world as we know it, where fear turns us
from joy, and live in a more real one:

who knows if the moon's
a balloon,coming out of a keen city
in the sky—filled with pretty people?
(and if you and i should

get into it,if they
should take me and take you into their balloon,
why then
we'd go up higher with all the pretty people

than houses and steeples and clouds:
go sailing
away and away sailing into a keen
city which nobody's ever visited,where

always
    it's
        Spring)and everyone's
in love and flowers pick themselves   (VII: 103)

Although this is a very early poem (*&*, 1925) and hence lacks the philosophical language that Cummings developed later to express his ideas, it does epitomize the essential quality of transcendence that permeates his vision. That language, to express this idea, includes by now such key terms as *above, under, depth, height,* and *beyond:*

for you are and i am and we are(above
and under all possible worlds)in love   (66: 464)

There are three or four areas of human thought and experience about which Cummings' speaker has any ideas: love, death, and time; the natural and the artificial; society and the individual; and dream and reality. Transcendence means freedom from limitations and has its source in a sinless universe. Each of these topics, therefore, involves an opposition that illustrates this general freedom in a particular way: love transcends death and time; the individual transcends the group; the natural transcends the artificial; and the dream is the true reality.

But it is a freedom to be achieved only by surrender, which is another word for love:

let it go—the
smashed word broken
open vow or
the oath cracked length
wise—let it go it
was sworn to
      go

let them go—the
truthful liars and
the false fair friends
and the boths and
neithers—you must let them go they
were born
      to go

let all go—the
big small middling
tall bigger really
the biggest and all
things—let all go
dear
      so comes love   (XXIX: 406)

It is a disciplined freedom, a transcendence won not without cost, a victory in one world which depends upon defeat in another:

what if a dawn of a doom of a dream
bites this universe in two,
peels forever out of his grave
and sprinkles nowhere with me and you?
Blow soon to never and never to twice
(blow life to isn't:blow death to was)
—all nothing's only our hugest home;
the most who die,the more we live   (XX: 401)

It is a living that grows out of a dying—"we've/such freedom such intense digestion so/ much greenness only dying makes us grow" (5: 354)—and it is a finding preceded by a losing—"we(by a gift called dying born)must grow/ deep in dark least ourselves remembering/ love only rides his year. / All lose, whole find" (XVI: 398).

So it follows that a complete involvement in death, time, and the swing of the seasons results, as far as natural limitations are concerned, in a transformation, and acceptance becomes transcendence:

> i will wade out
>   till my thighs are steeped in burning flowers
> I will take the sun in my mouth
> and leap into the ripe air
>   Alive
>   with closed eyes
> to dash against darkness
>   in the sleeping curves of my body
> Shall enter fingers of smooth mastery
> with chasteness of sea-girls
>   Will i complete the mystery
>   of my flesh
> I will rise
>   After a thousand years
> lipping
> flowers
>   And set my teeth in the silver of the moon   (XI: 139)

As far as manmade limits are concerned—social conventions, clocks and calendars, sterile abstractionist philosophies, religions and sciences, and the world of "reality"—he will have none of them, transcendence here being a matter of detachment:

> when the oak begs permission of the birch
> to make an acorn—valleys accuse their
> mountains of having altitude—and march
> denounces april as a saboteur
>
> then we'll believe in that incredible
> unanimal mankind(and not until)   (22: 442)

For mass man has inverted natural process—the fertile and life-perpetuating cycle of living, dying, and being reborn—and, as a result, he has created an artificial and unreal world for himself to exist in—where he neither lives nor dies. But a true individual, a man as opposed to mankind, is a natural and miraculous phenomenon; he is on a par, in the world of Cummings' speaker, with trees and mountains and flowers:

so many selves(so many fiends and gods
each greedier than every)is a man
(so easily one in another hides;
yet man can,being all,escape from none)

. . . . .

—how should a fool that calls him "I" presume
to comprehend not numerable whom?   (11: 435)

An individual is a mystery as the mob is a lie:

—when skies are hanged and oceans drowned,
the single secret will still be man   (XX: 401)

As a consequence, it is clear that such a character prefers the natural
to the manmade in traditional romantic style: birds sing sweeter than
books tell how (LIV: 423); beware of heartless them, for given a scalpel
they dissect a kiss (XVI: 398); soul and heart are truer guides than
mind:

three wealthy sisters swore they'd never part:
Soul was(i understand)
seduced by Life;whose brother married Heart,
now Mrs Death.   Poor Mind   (23: 442)

"Poor Mind"!—Soul and Heart are involved in the forces of life and
death, and hence are performing vital functions, while Mind, sterile
and alone, remains in an abstracted state of nonexistence. Mind seems
to be the villain of Cummings' drama, the Satan of his Eden, the snake
in the garden, the substitute for original sin which we notice was absent from the universe of his speaker. Mind for him is, when separated
from heart and soul, that in man which prevents him from keeping in
harmony with natural process, which causes him to look around the
corners of the seasons and fear what he sees, which makes him seek
answers to unanswerable questions, and which fabricates lies and machines and bureaucracies to protect him from reality.
    Cummings' persona sees nothing noble or tragic in man's intellectual

strivings, for they cut him off from truth and cause him to live in a desert land of fear and frustration:

> "summer is over
> —it's no use demanding
> that lending be giving;
> it's no good pretending
> befriending means loving"
> (sighs mind:and he's clever)
> "for all,yes for all
> sweet things are until"   (27: 443)

Heart answers with the simple truth that spring follows winter, and soul backs up heart by claiming that "now," or that which we can perceive immediately, can always be more than "forever," or that which we can only know by abstraction. Yet mind infects man with the disease of asking and of dissatisfaction:

> when man determined to destroy
> himself he picked the was
> of shall and finding only why
> smashed it into because   (XXVI: 404)

But, in echo of Whitman's speaker, Cummings' persona claims that

> life is more true than reason will deceive

> .   .   .   .   .

> the mightiest meditations of mankind
> cancelled are by one merely opening leaf   (LII: 421)

It is a mistake to conclude that he contradicts himself here—on the grounds that, if we took such statements seriously we would have to prefer the leaf to Cummings' poetry—because he does not mean, when he says books are inferior to birds and trees, that poems are products of mind. (Poems are natural products too because they come from a whole man in tune with nature's musics (XLVII: 418), and they are in competition with flowers and sunsets.)

Therefore, since mind wants to make static the moving and finish the never-ending, its dominance creates for man an artificial world. Moneys and societies and wars are the results; they are all abstractions and they all destroy man's capacity for life. Collective man in the modern world, as our sociologists and psychologists have recently discovered, feels only what he is supposed to feel, acts only as others expect him to act, and thinks only what is proper to think; the result is automatism, mass anxiety, and universal restlessness. But Cummings' speaker, curiously enough, has known this all along: man has needs and desires that can be ignored only at the cost of killing his psychic life; and the tyranny of the majority, which Mill analyzed so keenly a hundred years ago, is the chief target of Cummings' satire. Nor are these needs and desires the indiscriminate and suicidal products of a romantic egoism, as a literary moralist like Ivor Winters would have us believe; they have rather to do with the fundamental necessity to create, to make things. And it is this necessity that our commercial culture, with its emphasis upon manipulating rather than making, denies.

The world of the stock response, the conditioned reflex, and the public opinion poll; the world of salesmanship, advertising, and ballyhoo; the world of the movies, the radio, and television; the world of the mass circulation picture magazine, the digest, and the comic book; the world of politics, economic security, and of New Deals, Fair Deals, New Looks, and the Five-Year Plans; the world, in short, in which most of us live—this is, for Cummings' speaker, the "really unreal world," the "unworld" of the manmade hoax, the product of mind. Who are we, therefore, to say it is real?—to charge that Cummings exaggerates the importance of love?—to claim that prestige and security, our primary objectives in life, are more valuable than self-reliance and true self-consciousness?

He is right; he is right if all our sages, saints, and prophets are right: and we are wrong and all our politicians, admen, and literary theologians are wrong.

Salvation, remedy, cure—coinages of a sick world—are to be found in love, for "though hate were why men breathe—/ . . . / love is the

whole and more than all" (34: 375). Love is the courage to hope, the
determination to be oneself, the ability to dream, the capacity for surrender, and the desire for life:

lovers are mindless . . .

. . . . .

lovers are those who kneel   (XXIII: 402)

*

love is the every only god

who spoke this earth so glad and big
even a thing all small and sad
man,may his mighty briefness dig

for love beginning means return   (38: 378)

If Mind is the dehumanized Satan of Cummings' universe, Love is its
humanized Christ.

Thus the world that love creates is the reality of our speaker's world:
a world of dream, of the creative imagination, of the felt truth, of wisdom rather than knowledge, of spiritual strength rather than physical
prowess, of value rather than fact—a world in which is "so awake what
waking calls asleep" (11: 435). It is where time is timeless and all questions are answered; the world that we can reach, paradoxically enough,
by consenting to live in time without question:

no heart can leap,no soul can breathe
but by the sizeless truth of a dream
whose sleep is the sky and the earth and the sea.
For love are in you am in i are in we   (66: 465)

*

from some complete existence of to dream
into complete some dream of to exist
a stranger who is i awakening am.   (XIX: 400)

The "someones" and "everyones" of the world sleep their dream while the "noones" and "anyones" dream their sleep (29: 370), for what this world calls sleep is the artist's awake:

> and it is dawn
> the world
> goes forth to murder dreams . . . .
>
> .   .   .   .   .
>
> in the mirror
> i see a frail
> man
> dreaming
> dreams
> dreams in the mirror   (IV: 42–43)

Dream is the world of transcendence—although not, as I have shown, a specifically Christian world—the world of unconscious and spontaneous power, of the night, the moon, and the stars.

The key terms that Cummings has developed to express the various aspects of this world are *mystery, miracle, secret,* and *magic.* Forever and when are now, whereas in the unworld they are never and until; the place is here, whereas in the unworld it is where. The verb is am, while in the unworld it is was; to be equals born, while in the unworld it is made. It is the world of end, begin, and return *vs.* the unworld of must, shall, and can't; of new and young *vs.* same; of yes *vs.* if, un, non, but, unless, almost, and since; of who and each *vs.* which; of why *vs.* because; of dare *vs.* fear; of give *vs.* keep, have, and lend; of fail *vs.* succeed; of sing and see *vs.* say and stare; of living and dying *vs.* death and undying; of alive *vs.* it and thing; of immeasurable *vs.* measurable; and so on.

This is the vocabulary and the language that have become Cummings' trade-mark even more than his typographical arrangements, not only because they are the vehicle of a conception of the world which is rare in modern poetry but also because they reflect a unique style characterized by the systematic and wholesale transformation of verbs and adjectives into nouns. It is as if, in order to transform the world, a transformation of the word were required. The reader of Cummings, however, soon adjusts himself to this manner of expression and learns to accept its use as perfectly necessary and natural. At the same time the reader experiences the thrill of discovery; if one of the poet's functions is to revitalize the language, this is a poetic achievement that makes a real contribution to our lyric tradition. The idea is inseparable from its expression, and Cummings thus makes us see old values in a fresh and perceptive way; he has developed a conceptual vehicle of delicate precision and, in his later work especially, can express his values in a vivid, compressed, and exciting fashion, unobtrusively and without the danger of flatness which a gnomic poet such as Frost, for example, is always skirting. For Cummings' language is a grammatical code that achieves significance only in context; but since each of its terms means exactly what it seems to say, it is a code that requires no key for its deciphering.

Take, for instance, Frost's excellent "Choose Something Like a Star," wherein the perceptive Yankee speaker asks a star to

> Say something to us we can learn
> By heart and when alone repeat.

It is a partially humorous, partially serious request, and continues on in this delightful vein:

> Talk Fahrenheit, talk Centigrade.
> Use language we can comprehend.

It concludes more seriously and quite effectively, but somewhere just this side of prose:

> It asks of us a certain height,
> So when at times the mob is swayed
> To carry praise or blame too far,
> We may choose something like a star
> To stay our minds on and be staid.

As usual, we are impressed by the absolute rightness of this speaker's truth, with the orderly yet imaginative and witty development of his thought, and, also as usual, with the exciting things he does with the prosaic when by all rights he ought to be stumbling over his iambic foot.

We value Frost's skill, and modern poetry can ill spare it, but Cummings' is of another kind entirely:

> morsel miraculous and meaningless
>
> secret on luminous whose selves and lives
> imperishably feast all timeless souls
>
> (the not whose spiral hunger may appease
> what merely riches of our pretty world
> sweetly who flourishes,swiftly which fails
>
> but out of serene perfectly Nothing hurled
> into young Now entirely arrives
> gesture past fragrance fragrant;a than pure
>
> more signalling of singular most flame
> and surely poets only understands)
> honour this loneliness of even him
>
> who fears and eyes lifts lifting hopes and hands
> —nourish my failure with thy freedom:star
>
> isful beckoningly fabulous crumb   (71: 326)

(Ignoring, for the present purpose, such otherwise crucial matters as distortion of word order, grammatical displacement, spacing, capitalization, parentheses, punctuation, and the like, we notice here such characteristic examples of Cummings' conceptual language as *miraculous, secret, timeless souls, not, fails, who, which, Nothing, young Now, fears, hopes, failure, freedom,* and *isful*. While Frost converts his star into a symbol of aspiration and guidance through the medium of a language characterized by normal constructions, just touched by rhyme and meter to give it a musical resonance, Cummings does the same thing through a language that he himself has partially invented and that is barely held together by the rhyme and the meter.)

Although we can infer most of the meaning in such a poem by reading the work itself attentively, it does help a great deal to have a larger acquaintance with Cummings' terms and ideas before attempting to do so. Since the star epitomizes for him the real world of dream and imagination, it is "miraculous" and "secret"; it is an aspect of timelessness. It is a "not," a thing of no importance in the unworld, of no category and having no label; it comes out of "Nothing," which is Cummings' equivalent for the world beyond death or his Nirvana, into "young Now," being alive and realized in the perpetual present of sensing and feeling and imagining. It lifts eyes and hands, converting fears into hopes. The speaker, being a poet and referring to all true individuals as poets, appeals to this star to transform his failure as a citizen of the unworld into the freedom of the dream world—this star, which is "isful" in being alive and pulsating with the mystery of life.

All this is accomplished without the plainness that results from Frost's proclivity for overt statement, and, because it requires continual translation in the process of reading, it makes for greater dramatic impact, as is the case with symbols. Just as Frost's work is always in danger of flatness, so Cummings is always in danger of obscurity; but neither of these poets falls into his own particular trap very often. Cummings at his best can be read aloud just as easily and delightfully as Frost, for his obscurity—simply a matter of our not being used to hearing language transformed in this way—dissolves once the technique is grasped. In changing the grammatical forms of words, he never changes their root significance: "isful," for example, can become an adjective without too much imaginative effort—once the fact has been grasped that a verb is being used as a noun and that the noun is being used as an adjective by the addition of an appropriate suffix—because its meaning as referring to the quality of being alive is obviously dependent upon the original meaning of the verb.

The fact that Cummings has come to use these grammatical shifts so frequently and with so systematic a correspondence to his moral and philosophical views, is what necessitates such elucidation as I have attempted. His use of these forms was rather negligible in his first three volumes—*Tulips and Chimneys* (1922), & [*And*] (1925), and *is* 5 (1926) —but became more pronounced in the middle three volumes—*VV* [*ViVa*] (1931), *No Thanks* (1935), and *New Poems* [from *Collected Poems*] (1938)—and has become one of the most dominant features of his work in the last three volumes—*50 Poems* (1940), *1 x 1* [*One Times One*] (1944), and *Xaipe: Seventy-One Poems* (1950).

The development of his poetic thought, then, has been rather an unfolding than a series of climaxes and new directions; his later thought, indeed implicit in his earlier work, simply becomes fuller and more precisely and accurately expressed. There is more conceptual vigor, seriousness, and originality in his later work and less of the aesthetic posing and derivative wit that characterized many of his earlier poems. This maturity is due to the simultaneous and mutual growth of the quality of his thought and the skill required to express it in a fresh and personal manner. It is wrong, therefore, to say that Cummings has not developed, that he has remained fixed in his adolescent attitudes; he has deepened and extended and confirmed them, and he has learned to put them forth with greater impact. No man who has retained and strengthened the visions of his youth with such singular integrity for almost sixty years can be accused of perpetual adolescence. He has simply practiced what he has been preaching all along—that the vision of the world that childhood gives us is the truest we shall ever know—and it is only our commitment to a sobered adult view that makes us minimize the importance of an imagination such as his.

III / If the character and thought of this speaker represent select aspects of the character and thought of its creator, so also do the subjects he dwells upon and the circumstances that give rise to his dramatic responses represent select aspects of the poet's actual environment. As the speaker, in other words, is a created persona, so his subjects and situations form a created world of images. And here also, taking them up in the order of their importance, we will learn as much from the omissions as from the inclusions.

Love always was and still is Cummings' chief subject of interest. The traditional lyric situation, representing the lover speaking of love to his lady, has been given in our time a special flavor and emphasis by Cummings. Not only the lover and his lady, but love itself—its quality, its value, its feel, its meaning—is a subject of continuing concern to our speaker.

Cummings is furthermore in the habit of associating love, as a subject, with the landscape, the seasons, the times of day, and with time and death—as poets have always done in the past. Love and lovers, not only traditionally but also as a logical consequence of the speaker's thought, are seen against the background of, and in harmony with, nature and natural process:

> trees
>   were in(give
> give)bud when to me
> you
> made for by love
> love said did
> o no yes   (XLIX: 419)

Love and lovers, alone and associated with natural process, account for the subjects of well over one-fifth of Cummings' poems.

Only a little less important numerically are those poems dealing with the external world as a subject in itself, which includes not only the traditional matter of nature and natural process but also—and this is a characteristic of Cummings' poetry that distinguishes him as a modern of a certain kind—street and city scenes. However, natural scenes always outnumber these latter, which show signs of diminishing in importance as Cummings develops. Urban interest was higher in *Tulips and Chimneys* (1922) and in *&* (1925) than in the volumes from *is 5* (1926) to *50 Poems* (1940), and almost disappears in *1 x 1* (1944) and in *Xaipe* (1950).

He is fond of linking these subjects, so that he writes many poems

that deal with a season plus a landscape plus a time of day, or a street
scene plus a season plus a time of day:

> Paris: this April sunset completely utters
> utters serenely silently a cathedral
> before whose upward lean magnificent face
> the streets turn young with rain   (V: 75–76)

(Love, the external world, and their various relationships account for
the subjects of almost half of Cummings' poems.)

(Ideas constitute his next most significant subject.) It is frequently said
that Cummings, happy primitive and sensuous anti-intellectual that he
is, is undistinguished as a thinker. Whatever we may think of such a
lack in a lyric poet, it is simply not true that he shares this quality with,
say, Campion or Lovelace. The more one reads the complete poems, the
more one is impressed by the relatively high proportion of nondramatic
and satirical poems, the subjects of which are exclusively values and concepts, to say nothing of the many dramatic poems that express or imply
abstract ideas in connection with the thought and character of the
speaker as he responds to a variety of circumstances.

On the surface this may seem contradictory, for are not Cummings'
poems characterized by their romantic, "let's live suddenly without
thinking" (IX: 121), bias? We are dealing here with the fundamental
irony of much of modern art which, as we have been told often enough,
has been obsessed with the problem of fitting a three-dimensional reality
into two-dimensional forms (cf. *Him* I.ii. p. 12). How can our novelists write novels devoid of traditionally shaped plots and still be writing
novels? How can our poets write poems that capture the chaos of the
modern world in poems that are not chaotic themselves? To create an
effect of simultaneity in a language that is necessarily sequential, to
damn abstraction in words that are necessarily abstractions—this is the
next-to-impossible task which Joyce, Woolf, Stein, Hemingway, Eliot,
William Carlos Williams, Cummings, and a host of others have set
for themselves.

However this may be, one can fight ideas only with other ideas if one wishes to write at all. The fact remains that Cummings, from *is* 5 (1926) on, reveals a steady concern with ideas and has developed a conceptual vocabulary for expressing them, as we have had ample occasion to demonstrate:

> who were so dark of heart they might not speak,
> a little innocence will make them sing;
> teach them to see who could not learn to look
>
> .   .   .   .   .
>
> . . . the proud power of himself death immense
> is not so as a little innocence   (51: 456)

The apparent contradiction is easily resolved once we see that Cummings is not against "thinking" in the sense of having moral values and making moral choices, for he is nothing if not a moralist. It is rather that he is against "thinking" in the sense of allowing the brain to usurp or thwart the rightful functions of the heart and the senses—"Hearts being sick,Minds nothing can" (54: 314)—an attitude that he shares with another non-anti-intellectual poetic moralist, George Meredith. Those poems devoted exclusively to concepts make up just one-sixth of Cummings' work as a whole.

We have already discussed the detachment from the normal world of work and routine of Cummings' persona, and we may note here, in relation to his third most important poetic subject matter, the conspicuous absence of interest in marriage, children in relation to parents, working, groceries, bills, illness, diapers, dishes, laundry, worry, mundane responsibility, and social life. There are few poems on these subjects in the lot, and one of them disqualifies itself because its speaker is obviously an antimask, a character separate and distinct from Cummings' usual persona:

> . . . a feller tries
> to hold down the fifty bucks per
> job with one foot and rock a
>
> cradle with the other)   (XIII: 175)

This world is for our speaker a world lost in fear and anxiety, a waste-land, an inferno. Not because having children and responsibilities is deadening to the human soul, but rather because the fear and anxiety that these things engender in a competitive industrial society do kill us. To have children means to want a job, to get a job means to be afraid of losing it, and to be afraid of losing it means to want a better one. Since most of the jobs available today commit us to routine, our typists, clerks, junior executives, salesmen, and factory workers are reduced to hirelings, yea-sayers, and automatons. And in elevating economic security to a position of supreme value, we have become slaves altogether.

Almost as if in compensation, the world that does excite our speaker's interest might be termed the demimonde. It is made up of bars, restaurants, sports arenas, brothels, burlesque theaters, and nightclubs; and it is peopled by bums, whores, pimps and madams, fairies, lesbians, Turks, chorus girls and belly-dancers, torch singers, prize fighters, gangsters, circus acrobats and clowns, toughs, Negroes, itinerant ped-dlars and repairmen, Chinese laundrymen and Yiddish tailors. It is the world of the modern artist in self-imposed exile from modern industrial society; it is the world of Rimbaud and Toulouse-Lautrec, of Picasso's early paintings and of Hemingway's early stories.

The reason for the modern artist's interest in this world is that those who inhabit it are similarly dispossessed and alienated from the bour-geois world, are similarly without a stable socio-economic role:

If you can't eat you got to

smoke and we aint got
nothing to smoke:come on kid

let's go to sleep   (3: 353)

It is also a world where the poet's persona finds the emotional honesty and physical vitality that he misses in the sterile world of the middle class, and it is a world that has become something of a literary tradition of the modern period wherein relief is sought from the aridity of con-temporary civilization among the undercivilized and the outlawed.

This subject, however, which accounted for a very high proportion of poems in Cummings' first two volumes, has gradually diminished since *is 5* (1926), until by now it occupies our speaker only rarely.

Perhaps as a function of this decrease, there is a gradually increasing interest in people—as types or as separate individuals—which begins to appear in *is 5* (1926), continues through *New Poems* (1938), and is most prominent from *50 Poems* (1940) on. These are frequently other performers, artists, and poets whom the speaker admires—Buffalo Bill, Joe Gould, Paul Rosenfeld, Paul Draper, Ford Madox Ford, Jimmy Savo, the early Picasso, Aristide Maillol, Peter Munro Jack, and others; or anonymous old men and women; or types he dislikes—generals, presidents, Cambridge ladies, tourists, salesmen, and captains of industry. Not being content to praise or blame in the abstract—unlike Sandburg, he is incapable of singing the praises of Mankind or of The People—and not being the snob he is often taken to be, Cummings is at his best when he celebrates a specific human being he has known:

> rain or hail
> sam done
> the best he kin
> till they digged his hole   (XXVIII: 405)

It is therefore simply not true that our speaker is a child against the world, that he is against everything and everybody except himself; he is as prone to praise as he is to blame, and, in spite of his distaste for crowds (he is constitutionally shy, just as he has reported his mother as being), he has many friends, he has parents (a characteristic that too few personae of modern poetry share), he has his lady, and he is aware of people around him. But these constitute a personal society, the only kind that is real for him.

The "really unreal world," the world built upon a "colossal hoax of clocks and calendars," the world of "mostpeople" is comprised of such subjects as war, national affairs, commercialism, and politics. This is the hell of our speaker's universe; the limbo of "a not alive undead too nearishness," an "idiotic monster of negation," a "collective pseudo-

beast"; the unworld of hate, greed, bureaucracy, stupidity, and char-
latanism. Interest in these subjects is significantly almost nonexistent in
his first two volumes, but develops in *is 5* (1926) and *VV* (1931)—

the first president to be loved by his
bitterest enemies" is dead

the only man woman or child who wrote
a simple declarative sentence with seven grammatical
errors "is dead"
beautiful Warren Gamaliel Harding　　　　　　　　(XXVII: 242)

An interest in these same subjects, almost entirely lacking in *No
Thanks* (1935), *New Poems* (1938), and *50 Poems* (1940), reappears
again in *1 x 1* (1944) and *Xaipe* (1950):

o to be in finland
now that russia's here)　　　　　　　　　　　　　(43: 452)

The ebb and flow of this interest mirrors our recent national history,
but in a uniquely characteristic way. It was not until after the First
World War that Cummings began to look at the national scene, and
many of his subsequent poems reflect the problems arising out of the
Depression:

(hutch)hutchinson says sweet guinea
pigs do it it buy uh cupl un
wait　　　　　　　　　　　　　　　　　　　　(XVII: 235)

And then, after a lapse, he writes of war and politics once again, on the
heels of the Second World War:

　. . . it took
a nipponized bit of
the old sixth

avenue
el;in the top of his head:to tell

him　　　　　　　　　　　　　　　　　　　　(XIII: 396)

What is uniquely characteristic of Cummings' interest in war and politics is the fact that his persona never had a good word to say either for the bureaucracy of the New Deal, or for those of Socialism, Communism, and Fascism—and this at a time when many of our outstanding novelists and poets were feeling very strongly the tug of a newly awakened social conscience, after a lot of talk in the 1920's about art. He is the polar opposite, in this, of a MacLeish, a Spender, a Pound, or a Dos Passos, and I dare say that the Poetry of History, as Karl Shapiro has recently argued, is ready to be superseded, along with the Poetry of the Religion of Art, by just plain poetry. Cummings, for example, actually went to Russia in the early 1930's, when Communism was the Hope of Mankind for egghead and peasant alike, and saw only oppression, sterility, and death—so much so that, when he got back to the bourgeois West, he almost knelt and kissed the ground! And he was practically alone at that time among the avant-garde not only in expressing his revulsion, but also by doing it in print.

The truth of the matter is that, for Cummings as well as for his speaker, what most of us call the "real" world simply does not exist, not necessarily and just because it is evil but rather because it is external and abstract. No one can feel History, or see a Government; they are made up, they are fake. The artist's country is himself, and treason or loyalty have meaning only in relationship to that citizenship; people who live in the unworld, since they exist in terms of that world, change when that world changes, succeed when that world succeeds, and collapse when that world collapses (witness the mass suicide of businessmen after the Crash). They are dead because they are not true to themselves. He makes no compromise, then, on this score:

> my specialty is living said
> a man(who could not earn his bread
> because he would not sell his head)
>
> squads right impatiently replied
> two billion pubic lice inside
> one pair of trousers(which had died)   (11: 339)

The poet, then, creates the character, thought, and world of his persona out of internal necessity, and the critic need only ask if out of this necessity are created serious and beautiful poems. A sensual mystic, Cummings is not of this world. If he is immature, it is the immaturity of a visionary; his persona represents no mere aesthetic pose.

Everything written is as good as it is dramatic. It need not declare itself in form, but it is dramatic or nothing. A least lyric alone may have a hard time, but it can make a beginning, and lyric will be piled on lyric till all are easily heard as sung or spoken by a person in a scene—in character, in setting. By whom, where and when is the question. By a dreamer of the better world out in a storm in autumn; by a lover under a window at night.

—Robert Frost, Foreword to *A Way Out*

CHAPTER TWO # action

We inquire now into the kinds of responses that Cummings portrays his speaker as acting out in consequence of endowing him with a certain character, set of beliefs, and subject matter. And the kinds of responses that a speaker may experience in a lyric are, commonly, to praise, to blame, to persuade, to react emotionally, to describe, to meditate, to reflect, and to set forth or argue a proposition.

I / Before going on to examine each in detail, there are several things to be said about the kinds of responses in which Cummings' speaker is involved. In the first place, contrary to the common opinion that he writes only songs or satires, his work exhibits a surprisingly wide variety. This distinguishes him from many of our other first-rate contemporary poets, such as Frost or Thomas or Eliot, whose speakers are almost always represented as reflecting or meditating. There are few modern poets who can equal Cummings in the dexterity with which he writes now a satire, now a poem of praise, now a reflective lyric, now a description, or now a poem of persuasion.

In the second place, and conversely, the one form in which he shows no interest whatever is the poem of meditation. The absence of this type, which is characterized by conflict and struggle in that the speaker is represented in the process of deliberating over a decision he must make or reasoning out a problem he must face, is logical enough, however. His is a poetry of resolution rather than of conflict, and the distinctive trait of Cummings' persona is his certainty, his freedom from doubt and anxiety, his transcendence of ambivalence and paradox. Unlike Thomas, he feels no guilt for his mortal flesh; unlike Eliot, he does not strive to embrace a religious tradition in a secular world; unlike Frost, he feels no pull between the desire to let go and the need to have control. If he had stopped by those woods on that snowy evening, he would in all probability have stayed there to enjoy the wintry trance which Frost's speaker was so scrupulous in resisting.

It is the meditative poem, it seems to me, that is most typical of our age (so typical indeed that some of our critics are trying to interpret the whole of our poetic tradition in terms of this one form); and it is this form that Cummings avoids completely. An instructive contrast may be found in comparing Donne's Holy Sonnet XIII, "What If This Present Were the World's Last Night?" with Cummings' "what if a much of a which of a wind" (XX: 401). We all know that Donne has exerted a striking influence on the kind of modern poetry that I am counterposing to Cummings'; and Donne's sonnet deals in a characteristically meditative fashion with a characteristically religious subject. Its speaker suddenly imagines that the Day of Judgment is at hand and asks his soul if it can bear to face the image of Christ crucified which he bears engraved upon his heart. Can that suffering face frighten you? he asks; can that tongue, which prayed for the forgiveness of His enemies, adjudge you unto Hell? The implied answer is, of course, yes! But he continues on to assuage the horror he has aroused in his soul by saying, "No, no." As an ugly face signifies harshness, so a beautiful one bespeaks mercy. Since, therefore, the image of Christ is beautiful, it will be "piteous."

The essential structural characteristic of this poem is that it reverses its direction as its speaker considers first one alternative solution to the problem raised at the beginning—being damned through unworthiness —and then the opposite alternative—being redeemed, in spite of unworthiness, by the infinite mercy of Christ. And the point is that, although the ending is affirmative, the negative alternative is entertained as a serious possibility. With Cummings it is quite otherwise; he asks the question and then answers it affirmatively, thus bypassing the negative alternative altogether:

> what if a much of a which of a wind
> gives the truth to summer's lie;
> bloodies with dizzying leaves the sun
> and yanks immortal stars awry?
> Blow king to beggar and queen to seem
> (blow friend to fiend:blow space to time)
> —when skies are hanged and oceans drowned,
> the single secret will still be man

If the world blows up entirely, he is saying in effect, and if all that we derive support from in this world vanishes, the essential values of the transcendent world will remain untouched:

> —all nothing's only our hugest home;
> the most who die,the more we live

The effect of Donne's poem is dramatic, for its speaker, talking to himself, frightens himself with the negative alternative before he arrives at the positive; the effect of Cummings' poem is rhetorical, for its speaker, talking probably to his lady, calmly announces the affirmative without taking the negative seriously—the possibility that the destruction of this world will leave us, as in MacLeish's "The End of the World," confronting an absolute blank. In this, Cummings is certainly not akin to the metaphysical spirit (with its "unified sensibility," and "reconciliation of opposites") of seventeenth- and twentieth-century poetry; he is rather more like the Elizabethan lyricists with their tuneful proclivity for praise, persuasion, and doctrine. Campion's "What If a Day, Or a Month, Or a Year?" is a case in point. The speaker here, as in Cummings' poem, is apparently addressing someone else, and, although the thought comes out quite differently than in Cummings, the form is the same. It involves question and answer without a consideration of the alternative:

> What if a day, or a month, or a year
> Crown thy delights with a thousand sweet contentings?
> Cannot a chance of a night or an hour
> Cross thy desires with as many sad tormentings?
>> Fortune, honor, beauty, youth
>> Are but blossoms dying;
>> Wanton pleasure, doting love
>> Are but shadows flying.

Nevertheless, granted this significant exception, there is little else that Cummings does not choose to do, and to do often and well, with poetic forms. By far the largest proportion of his poems is descriptive, amounting to almost one-fourth of his work as a whole. Although such poems were more frequent in his first two volumes, *Tulips and Chimneys* (1922) and *&* (1925), they appear fairly frequently in *No Thanks* (1935), *New Poems* (1938), and *50 Poems* (1940). There are few descriptive poems, however, in *is 5* (1926), *VV* (1931), and *Xaipe* (1950). In *1 x 1* (1944) there are practically none.

Almost as high, in proportion to the work as a whole, is the incidence of poems of praise and eulogy, which appear frequently in *Tulips and Chimneys* (1922), less often in *&* (1925), gradually more so in *is 5* (1926), *VV* (1931), *No Thanks* (1935), and *New Poems* (1938), and most often in the last three volumes. Correspondingly, the satirical poem, which was practically nonexistent in the first two volumes, appears in *is 5* (1925) and has been predominant ever since, averaging almost one-fifth of the complete poems.

Poems of reflection show a tendency to diminish in the later volumes, as do poems of persuasion, each of which accounts for an eighth of the work as a whole. Taken in connection with the increasing usage of poems of praise, do not these facts perhaps indicate that the speaker of Cummings' poems is turning more and more outward to his listener, who is usually his lady, and that, in doing so, he is becoming more interested in revealing her admirable qualities than in pointing things out to her and telling her things?

Description, praise and eulogy, satire, reflection, and persuasion, then, are the kinds of responses that Cummings' persona is most frequently portrayed as enacting, and in that order. And these poems account for almost 90 per cent of the total, the rest being a numerically, if not a relatively, substantial scattering of poems of proposition and emotion.

It remains now to consider Cummings' artistic habits in handling each of these forms.

II / The poem of description is organized to represent the speaker's impression of some dominant physical quality in a character, object, scene, place, or event; and it is, as we have seen, Cummings' most common form. A large portion of his poetic activity may be characterized as perceiving and rendering perception for its own sake—which is not surprising in a poet who is also a painter. But it is perception with a difference: Cummings is most interested in absolute accuracy, and in his effort to be true to the act of perception as it occurs he has developed many of the techniques for which he is so well known. Indeed, there is cause enough in his vision of life for such an attempt. Immediacy, freshness, directness, spontaneity, simultaneity and precision are theoretical concepts having a palpable effect upon why and how he writes descriptive poems. And the quantity of such poems re-emphasizes in turn the importance that he places upon the experience of sensation itself. It is not pure sensationalism, however, because of the very fact that Cummings regards such experience as having a moral value.

We may next inquire, then, into the things he describes and how he describes them. Times of the day, and particularly sunset-twilight-night-star-moon, which, as we shall see in the fourth chapter, constitute his chief symbolic cluster, share equal prominence with his dominant early interest in the demimonde. With regard to the former, he stresses those qualities—of silence, of orange, blue, yellow, red, and gold color, of contrasts between light and dark, of softness, vastness, calmness, and coolness, for example—which emphasize the erotic atmosphere of indolent, secret, lonely, magical, ghostly, and mysterious dreams, a transcendent world of love and fulfillment. He frequently sees the motion of the sun setting in terms of sound becoming silence, of bulk becoming fragility, of agony becoming serenity; he sees the light of the stars as writhing, bright, deep, and holy; and the motion of the moon rising, he sees as an acrobat in the trees, as a balloon bouncing in the sky:

mOOn Over tOwns mOOn
whisper
less creature huge grO
pingness

whO perfectly whO
flOat
newly alOne is
dreamest

oNLY THE MooN o
VER ToWNS
SLoWLY SPRoUTING SPIR
IT

(1: 277)

We may note here that the handling of capitalization suggests not only the roundness of the moon in the capitalized *O*'s of the first three stanzas, but also its gradual disappearance from view, leaving a shadowy spirit behind, as expressed in the capitalization of every letter except *o* in the last.

In sharp contrast to this dream world, he sees the vulgar, brawling, and blaring world of whores, restaurants, and nightclubs in terms of the click of billiard balls, the clink of glasses, of drinking, the smell of coffee, and the grossness of human flesh. He is far from being a naughty boy who thumbs his nose at prudes and takes a frank delight in the mechanics of sex. His descriptions of whores are frequently crass and shocking, but the qualities he dwells upon have more to do with their obscenity, their decay, the heavy drag and mortal weight of their bodies, the thickness and stickiness of their eyes, their coughing, their indignity, their gross and pathetic availability, their sickly ugliness, their tired and raucous voices, than with their pornographically appealing lusciousness. These are neither trembling virgins nor gossamer courtesans spun out of the harem of an adolescent's overheated imagination; they are lost ladies in league with death. And it is a mark of the humanity of Cummings' speaker that he finds them of such interest and describes them with such honest pity—and often with such humor.

Cummings' description of the seasons is next in importance. He shows a slight preference for spring-summer-rain over fall-winter-snow. The coming of spring is delicate and sloppy, sudden and immortal; what impresses him most is the way in which the world opens, at its arrival, into tints and tones and fragrances. Rain is new, fresh, young, dark, and soft, ghostly, slender, silent, slow, and dreamlike. Cummings often describes the snow as similar in these respects, which is strange when one considers how commonly it is seen as a form of chill dying, icy and tomblike. Fall, on the other hand, is seen as a season of shrinking, shriveling, and lifelessness: petals are murdered; trees are emptied and turn black; leaves drop, whirl down, and scratch across the dry earth; and birds desert their branches—it is an empty, dark, cold, and brittle time.

Scenery pieces, both urban and rural, are of equal importance. Our speaker is impressed by the sights and sounds of the city and its streets: the flashing on of street lamps; the horns of taxis; the conversation of people; the roar of the elevated trains; the wheezing of a hurdy-gurdy; the faces and streets and shops; carrousels; women hanging clothes in a tenement alleyway; houses; chimneys; roofs; pigeons and people in the park; dogs; children; bells; steeples; churches; and spires. New York, especially lower Manhattan, Boston, and Paris, are his cities. As for landscapes, he hears the tides of the sea moving and sees the wind dragging its waves, and writes frequently of trees, fields, flowers, rivers, forests, hills, and skies.

People and creatures come next. Although he sees an occasional horse or goat, he has a keener eye for smaller, even tiny, animals. He focuses, for example, on the eyes of a goldfish, the hop of a grasshopper, the leap of a cat, a chameleon changing color, a newly born horse or elephant, porcupines, an anteater, or birds; and it is largely their intricate capacity for complex movements and changes that fascinates him. Similarly, the people he describes are odd and out of the way: two old ladies sunning themselves in the park; an ugly and pathetic man; an old lady looking out of a window; an old flower man; a scissors-grinder; two old men on a bench; a man grinding a scythe-blade; a tatterdemalion.

III / Whom does our speaker praise and for what? The classical three phases of development evenly divide the nine volumes of poetry we are studying into three equal groups, and, it so happens, into three decades: *Tulips and Chimneys* (1922), *&* (1925), and *is* 5 (1926); *VV* (1931), *No Thanks* (1935), and *New Poems* (1938); *50 Poems* (1940), *1 x 1* (1944), and *Xaipe* (1950). In the first phase, our speaker mostly praises his lady for her erotic qualities, the beauty and desirability of her charms, and the wonderful effect that these have on him. In the second phase, praise of his lady declines and he centers on her spiritual qualities, while there is a corresponding increase in poems devoted to the praise of love and lovers in general, instead of just the lady herself in particular. In the third phase, praise of his lady enters a new state wherein her relationship to nature changes from one that compares her favorably with desirable natural phenomena to the more hyperbolic one of desirable natural phenomena being favorably compared to her. The praise of love and lovers doubles proportionately, and a new kind of subject gains in importance as a source of admiration. This source is the ideal poet-man in general and specific friends of the poet who exemplify, individually, that ideal.

Take, as an example of the first period, or phase, the following piece:

i have found what you are like
the rain,

       (Who feathers frightened fields
with the superior dust-of-sleep. wields

easily the pale club of the wind
and swirled justly souls of flower strike

the air in utterable coolness

deeds of green thrilling light
              with thinned

newfragile yellows
           lurch and press

—in the woods
        which
             stutter
                 and
                     sing

And the coolness of your smile is
stirringofbirds between my arms; but
i should rather than anything

have (almost when hugeness will shut
quietly) almost,
>   your kiss   (XII: 122–23)

The qualities he praises are the lady's person, her smile and kiss; and
the natural imagery used by way of comparison consists, typically, of
rain, coolness, twilight, flowers, woods, and birds.

As characteristic of the second period, or phase, notice the shift in
object and manner of praise:

love is the every only god

who spoke this earth so glad and big
even a thing all small and sad
man,may his mighty briefness dig

for love beginning means return
seas who could sing so deep and strong

one queerying wave will whitely yearn
from each last shore and home come young

so truly perfectly the skies
by merciful love whispered were,
completes its brightness with your eyes

any illimitable star   (38: 378)

Here the speaker begins with a general conceptual statement about the
creative power of love, and then applies that idea to the praise of his
lady, for she personifies or embodies love's creative power—with the
result that, instead of comparing her eyes to a star, her eyes are seen as
giving brightness to that very star, otherwise incomplete without her.
Two things have happened since the first period. He praises his lady
for spiritual rather than physical qualities, and he inverts the earlier
beauties-of-lady: beauties-of-nature relationship.

Also in this period, poems praising love and lovers begin to appear:

love's function is to fabricate unknownness

(known being wishless;but love,all of wishing)

though life's lived wrongsideout,sameness chokes oneness
truth is confused with fact,fish boast of fishing

and men are caught by worms(love may not care
if time totters,light droops,all measures bend
nor marvel if a thought should weigh a star
—dreads dying least;and less,that death should end)

how lucky lovers are(whose selves abide
under whatever shall discovered be)
whose ignorant each breathing dares to hide
more than most fabulous wisdom fears to see

(who laugh and cry)who dream,create and kill
while the whole moves;and every part stands still: (61: 321)

Love and lovers are praised for their spiritual strength, their ability to
transcend so-called civilization and the world of death and time, and to
rise up to the world of dream. We notice here typical samples of Cummings' conceptual vocabulary, which he has devised to express his
moral values in a fresh and vivid manner. These concepts include
sameness *vs.* oneness, known *vs.* unknownness, fact *vs.* truth, and fear *vs.*
dare. There is also his characteristic habit of inverting images—"fish
boast of fishing/ and men are caught by worms"—to indicate the up-
sidedown quality of natural relationships in the unworld.

Praise of the lady, in the third period, is marked by extreme hyper-
bole—

except in your
honour,
my loveliest,
nothing
may move may rest
—you bring

(out of dark the
earth)a
procession of
wonders . . .

```
who younger than
begin
are,the worlds move
in your
(and rest,my love)
honour                                        (XXXV: 409-10)
```

Also in the third period, praise of love and lovers increases (compare
the title poem of *1 x 1* at the end of that volume, LIV: 422–23; and
Xaipe, 66: 464–65). Praise of the ideal poet-man and his individual
manifestations, having appeared noticeably in the middle period, comes
into its own:

```
no man,if men are gods;but if gods must
be men,the sometimes only man is this
(most common,for each anguish is his grief;
and,for his joy is more than joy,most rare)          (XXII: 402)
```

He praises his father, Old Mr. Lyman, Goldberger, trapeze artists, Sam,
Peter Munro Jack, Paul Rosenfeld, Buffalo Bill, Picasso, Froissart, a
Breton sailor, Krassin, his mother, Joe Gould, Negroes, Paul Draper,
Jimmy Savo, Ford Madox Ford, Aristide Maillol, Nic, a Village scissors-
grinder, enlisted men, and Chaucer. He also praises beauty, spring,
innocence, nature, natural creatures and objects, and natural process.

IV / Satire, like comedy, is fast becoming a lost art in our age, so
strong is the current critical mode in favor of meditation, soul-search-
ing, and tragedy. In keeping with his unfashionable eccentricity on this
score, Cummings is a master of wit, in the simple sense of being funny,
and of the device of ridicule, in the sense of unreservedly making big
things look small. Satire depends, as we know, upon a sense of the
individual in society, and it is certainly a mistake to say, as has often
been done, that Cummings has no sense whatever of that vexed relationship. A satirist can write from within a given dominant group and

ridicule the nonconformists, as does Pope, or he can write from out-side the dominant group and ridicule the conformist, as does Byron. It is a matter of unfavorable contrast to a norm. Far from having no con-ception of the individual in society, Cummings is obsessed by this problem; but he writes about it from a different standpoint from that of most critics—whether left- or right-wingers—in asserting without question that any individual is better off apart from any group as things now stand. And this is because—since the only true moral goal in life is self-consciousness, self-reliance, and individual integrity—the group always tends to substitute its own manufactured product, its own stock response, and its own conditioned reflex for those of the individual. The artist's only true country is himself, and he is a citizen of im-mortality; it is the world of abstract loyalties, and its citizens, which are the objects of the ridicule of such an artist.

To speak more precisely, the subjects which are included in the cate-gory of national affairs constitute the chief butt of his satires—politics and politicians, celebrities, war, utopian theories, do-goodism, generals and admirals, chauvinism, presidents, bandwagoners, bigots, enthu-siasts, alarmists, bureaucrats and bureaucracy. These are sometimes treated in a general way and sometimes quite topically. These subjects did not attract Cummings' scorn until *is 5* (1926); in *No Thanks* (1935) his target shifts from war to Communism; Fascism comes in for its share of attack in *50 Poems* (1940); and in *1 x 1* (1944) and *Xaipe* (1950) war is again a central concern:

> when your honest redskin toma
> hawked and scalped his victim ,
>
> not to save a world for stalin
> was he aiming ;
>
> spare the child and spoil the rod
> quoth the palmist .   (45: 453-54)

Cummings, who had been to Russia in the 1930's and who had never felt very warm toward the USSR, felt sometime during the 1940's the irony we all now share regarding our unholy alliance with Russia during the Second World War.

Scientific commercialism and commercial scientism come next in importance as objects of satire, but they did not begin appearing until somewhat later, in *VV* (1931). Man as lord of the universe, man as technician, man as salesman, man as weight-lifter and record-breaker are images in direct opposition to man as individual, man as lover, man as artist, man as man. And fact *vs.* truth, knowledge *vs.* wisdom, physical prowess *vs.* physical strength, quantity *vs.* quality are the terms of the opposition. Cummings as satirist neither pities nor fears our American snake-oil vendors; he rather hates, scorns, and ridicules them:

a salesman is an it that stinks Excuse

Me whether it's president of the you were say
or a jennelman name misder finger isn't
important whether it's millions of other punks
or just a handful absolutely doesn't
matter and whether it's in lonjewray

or shrouds is immaterial it stinks

a salesman is an it that stinks to please   (IX: 394)

To trade on one's manufactured-for-the-occasion desire to help the customer according to the gospel of Saint Dale Carnegie, to sell toothpaste on the basis of laboratory proofs, to hawk a scientific theory of progress on the basis of philanthropical humanitarianism—these are anathema, the products of the damned and the merchandise of hell. Modern American advertising today, whether of the forum, the marketplace, the academy, or the laboratory, is an insult to human dignity; sloganism, testimonialism, and gadgetism are so common now that most of us can even bear it, and that, Cummings warns, is what is killing us.

The satire of people and types is almost of equal importance, and persists throughout the nine volumes. The Cambridge ladies, Salvation Army howlers, the superconventionalized and inhibited little Effie, the

smug and sexless graduate of an obscure university, lesbians and homosexuals, lady tourists in Venice, the sterile Miss Gay, Lord John Unalive
who made a fortune selling recorded musical culture to the millions,
little Mr. Big not busy Businessman, and a woman who complains that
birth was wicked and life is worse are the opposites of those people and
types whom Cummings praises, like old Mr. Lyman who, fresh from
a funeral, can still say there is enough in life for everybody, or the
Negro guitarist who cannot find it in his heart to hate this hurtful
world. The former, by contrast, are empty, dead, sexless, lifeless, dull,
damned, and without hope:

> the Cambridge ladies who live in furnished souls
> are unbeautiful and have comfortable minds
> (also, with the church's protestant blessings
> daughters, unscented shapeless spirited)
> they believe in Christ and Longfellow, both dead,
> are invariably interested in so many things—   (I: 58)

"Mostpeople" is a subject in itself, which, except for *is* 5 (1926) and
VV (1931), shows up in each volume. Neither an individual nor a type,
mostpeople is a huge and collective pseudo beast, a busy monster, an
incredible unanimal; in short, what mankind becomes "where freedom
is compulsory/ and only man is god"—a creature so completely
hemmed in by clocks, calendars, advertisements, slogans, loyalties, conventions, machines, and sundry other hoaxes being sold as sovereign
remedies to cure the disease of feeling and being, that it is made up of
parts that have ceased to exist and yet retain a kind of nonexistent
existence by virtue of their being absorbed in the whole:

> these people socalled were not given hearts
> how should they be?their socalled hearts would think
> these socalled people have no minds but if
> they had their minds socalled would not exist   (24: 366)

*

> Without a heart the animal
> is very very kind

so kind it wouldn't like a soul
and couldn't use a mind   (IV: 391)

Cummings has been accused of being egocentric and undemocratic,
but it is only because he has such an absolute conviction in the dignity
of man and the freedom of the human will that he can have such a hate
for conformity. If the individual were living in sullen revolt against the
tyranny of the majority, if flashes of dignity and courage were to be
seen illuminating the foggy collectivistic horizon, if gentleness and integrity and innocence were found in some unlikely Rotarian or Legion-
naire heart, then would Cummings cry out in pity and joy. But such a
hope would be even more sentimental than Cummings has been
accused of being. What prevents such sentiment in him is the unde-
niable horror of the fact that people are submitting everywhere volun-
tarily to slavery. And they like it! or at least they cannot face the fear
of disapproval and discomfort that motivates their sickly compromise.
Cummings' satire is grounded on an unshakable faith in the nobility
of the human spirit; not heredity, not environment, not circumstance,
not city hall are the causes of human degradation, but rather the cor-
rupt will, the will self-corrupted. If it is in man's power to choose—the
basic premise of human dignity—and to choose rightly, how can we
pity him when he consciously chooses wrongly out of fear? Pity is
caused by a stricter sense of human limitation and powerlessness than
Cummings can command.

Satire of the literati forms a small but substantial group of poems.
With the exception of his labeling Hemingway (26: 294) and Untermeyer (XI: 394), this is usually done without personal reference. His
butts are "wrongers who write what they are dine to live" (XXVI:
242), manifesto-blaring magazine starters (24: 293), and visiting British
poets of the leftist variety:

flotsam and jetsam
are gentlemen poeds
urseappeal netsam
our spinsters and coeds)

thoroughly bretish
they scout the inhuman
itarian fetish
that man isn't wuman

vive the millenni
um three cheers for labor
give all things to enni
one bugger thy nabor

(neck and senecktie
are gentlemen ppoyds
even whose recktie
are covered by lloyd's   (6: 354-55)

Cummings never had much patience with the modern psychologically
enlightened attitude toward sexual perversion. Homosexuals, especially
of the literary sort, receive nothing but his mockery, scorn, and ridicule
—especially British, communist, poetic homosexuals (*honi soit qui mal
y pense!*).

The latter poem amply illustrates several of Cummings' chief satirical
devices—the phonetically spelled or punning rhyme ("poeds-coeds,"
"ppoyds-lloyd's," etc.), the punning allusion ("neck and senecktie" is
from Horace's "labuntur anni; *nec* pietas moram/ rugis et instanti
senectae"), and the punning obscenity ("urseappeal netsam our spinsters and coeds," or, arse-appeal which nets them our lady culture-vul-
tures—and whose recktie, continuing on with the same telling ana-
tomical ridicule, are heavily insured).

Punning in general is his main source of witty ridicule:

what does little Ernest croon
in his death at afternoon?
(kow dow r 2 bul retoinis
wus de woids uf lil Oinis   (26: 294)

Not only the devastatingly punning parody in "cow thou art to bull
returnest" (cf. "A Psalm of Life"), but also the delicious mockery of

archaic language spelled as baby talk and of tough-guy language spelled phonetically, are responsible for the satirical effect here.

Another typical device is ironic self-revelation, by which Cummings allows a contemptible person to pronounce his bigotries in his own revoltingly characteristic language:

ygUDuh

> ydoan
> yunnuhstan
>
> ydoan o
> yunnuhstan dem   (VII: 393)

When transliterated back into standard English, this reads, in its entirety, "You've got to . . . you don't . . . you understand . . . you don't know . . . you understand them . . . you've got to get . . . you understand them dirty . . . you've got to get rid of . . . you don't know nothing . . . LISTEN, bud, LISTEN . . . them goddamn little yellow bastards, we're going to CIVILIZE them." Such an Anglo-Saxon, white-man's-burden pseudo humanitarianism, spoken in such an arrogant and scornful manner! Here everything depends, as this transliteration testifies, upon the phonetically rendered gutterisms: the speaker's character, his ridiculous but dangerous bigotry, his hatefulness.

A more obvious approach to ridicule is direct denunciation and invective: "hear/ ye!the godless are the dull and the dull are the damned" (13: 359). The unfavorable contrast and the unflattering comparison are used frequently. An unreal general, "(five foot five)/ neither dead/ nor alive," is pictured as standing "(in real the rain)" (42: 452); or mostpeople are compared, in traditional satiric fashion, to beasts, animals, monsters, and insects. Parody is another favorite device, Browning's "God's in His heaven" and "Oh, to be in England now that April's there" coming in for more than their share of service (e.g., IV: 169–70; XXVII: 183). Cummings also parodies the poetry of Kipling

(4: 335) and of Longfellow (26: 294), slogans, popular songs, nursery rhymes, spirituals, commercials, and patriotic oratory. Exaggeration, mock praise, sarcasm, and grotesquerie also account for many poisoned barbs:

> LONG LIVE that Upwardlooking
> Serene Illustrious and Beatific
> Lord of Creation,MAN:
> at a least crooking
> of Whose compassionate digit,earth's most terrific
>
> quadruped swoons into billiardBalls!   (VII: 227)

V / The poem of reflection represents its speaker as musing over or wondering about a certain person or type, place, event, or object, in an attempt somewhat tentatively and personally to interpret its significance by associating it with a chain of memories, by comparing it with something else, by converting it into a symbol, or by direct statement. Cummings' most frequent and persistently recurring reflective situation is one in which his persona describes and then thinks about one or more of his favorite images, such as spring, sunset, moon, star, tree, or bird, thereby transforming it into a symbol representing some concept or other out of which his world of values, or dream world, is built. Such is the case in the octave and sestet of the following sonnet:

> before the fragile gradual throne of night
> slowly when several stars are opening
> one beyond one immaculate curving
> cool treasures of silence
> (slenderly wholly
> rising, herself uprearing wholly slowly,
> lean in the hips and her sails filled with dream—
> when on a green brief gesture of twilight
> trembles the imagined galleon of Spring)
>
> somewhere unspeaking sits my life; the grim

clenched mind of me somewhere begins again,
shares the year's perfect agony.   Waiting

(always) upon a fragile instant when

herself me (slowly, wholly me) will press
in the young lips unearthly slenderness   (V: 118–19)

He wonders, in the spring, whether Death will touch an·old lady looking out of her window; when spring comes he is made a little dizzy by
numb thoughts coming to life; he understands what the rain means
when he touches his lady's hair; in fall and winter he challenges Death
and he makes a miracle of the snow; he senses the infinite nothingness
of night; he feels clumsy when he sees a new moon; and a star becomes holy in his vision.

Sex and whores, elements of his Toulouse-Lautrec demimonde, provided many reflective occasions in Cummings' first four volumes:

FRAN

should i entirely ask of god why
on the alert neck of this brittle whore
delicately wobbles an improbably distinct face,
and how these wooden big two feet conclude
happeningly the unfirm drooping bloated
calves
          i would receive the answer more
or less deserved, Young fellow go in peace.
which i do, being as Dick Mid once noted
lifting a Green River (here's to youse)
"a bloke wot's well behaved" . . . and always try
to not wonder how let's say elation
causes the bent eyes thickly to protrude—

or why her tiniest whispered invitation
is like a clock striking in a dark house   (V: 167)

These heavy ladies are the consorts of Death, perishing, final, and lost.
The street and city scene, similarly, provided reflective occasions only

in Cummings' first four volumes: "at the ferocious phenomenon of 5 o'clock i find myself gently decomposing in the mouth of New York" (IX: 149). The street is frequently the one through which he is walking on his way to visit his lady, or the one on which he is waiting expectantly for her to arrive; or again, it is where he lives under a stable and shares his room with a mouse, or a mysteriously empty apartment next to where he lives; or a street in Paris before a cathedral where trained animals are performing, or a place in a park near a carrousel where he once met a lover now gone.

There are several earlier reflective poems dealing with people and types, death, love, and time, and assorted landscapes: a twelve-year-old child with venereal disease; a queer old fellow with a yellow flower in his buttonhole; and a man he met on a hill overlooking Rome who reminded him of himself; a vision of paradise where timeless creatures dwell; a reflection on death, and one on the relationship between love and death; a scene where the seashore reminds him of sex; and a sense of personal foolishness provoked by looking at the view from a hill at Calchidas.

VI / As with the development of the poem of praise, we find three equal phases in the evolution of Cummings' handling of the poem of persuasion. This is organized by a situation in which the speaker is directing his remarks to another character within the poem. Speaking almost always to a woman of one kind or another, and most frequently to his lady, Cummings' persona is, in the first three volumes, either artfully posed and spitefully threatening her with his jealousy, flippantly scolding her about her infidelity, wittily demanding that she turn to him, or seriously but sentimentally pleading with her for a little love. He is alone with her in the presence of some night scene and asking for a kiss or an embrace, instructing her almost irreverently about the passage of time and love and of the value of sex, or, in a more serious vein, speaking consolingly of the transcendence of love over time and mind: "Come hither/ O thou, is love not death?" (I: 24); "consider O/

woman this/ my body" (I: 31); "if that he come receive/ him as your
lover sumptuously/ . . . for/ in his own land/ he is called death" (VI:
36); "it may not always be so; and i say/ that if your lips, which i have
loved, should touch/ another's . . . send me a little word" (I: 61); "if
i should sleep with a lady called death/ get another man with firmer
lips" (X: 121); "(ponder,darling,these busted statues" (XXX: 186).
One of the most successful of these early poems of persuasion is "since
feeling is first," in which the lady has apparently expressed a feeling of
inferiority in the presence of the speaker's superior mental powers, and
he turns to her consolingly and says:

> since feeling is first
> who pays any attention
> to the syntax of things
> will never wholly kiss you;
>
> wholly to be a fool
> while Spring is in the world
>
> my blood approves,
> and kisses are a better fate
> than wisdom
> lady i swear by all flowers. Don't cry
> —the best gesture of my brain is less than
> your eyelids' flutter which says
>
> we are for each other: then
> laugh, leaning back in my arms
> for life's not a paragraph
>
> And death i think is no parenthesis   (VII: 208–209)

This charming piece, implying as it does such delicate praise, expresses
one of our speaker's chief concepts regarding the relationship between
men and women—that a woman, in having a naturally intuitive and
life-giving nature, is closer to truth than a man with all his thoughts
and all his poems.
Such a seriously reverential and philosophical attitude toward the

lady becomes more frequent in the poems of persuasion of the middle
three volumes, in which the speaker is more concerned with explaining,
assuring, interpreting, and consoling than with scolding or entreating.
We're beyond death, let's despise cowardice, we're immortal, ask the
impossible of me, be glad and young: "what time is it i wonder never
mind/ consider rather heavenly things" (XIV: 233); "come a little further—why be afraid—/ here's the earliest star" (XLVIII: 257); "breathe
with me this fear/ (which beyond night shall go)/ remembering only
dare" (LIII: 261).

if you and i awakening

discover that(somehow
in the dark)this world has been
Picked,like a piece
of clover,from the green meadow of

time

lessness;quietly
                 turning
toward me the
guessable mirrors which your eyes are

You will communicate a little

more than twice all that
so
gently
while we were asleep while
we were each other disappeared . . .   (LXI: 265–66)

In the last three volumes this form of persuasion clearly becomes the
dominant mode: "we've/such freedom such intense digestion so/ much
greenness only dying makes us grow" (5: 354); "deeds cannot dream
what dreams can do/—time is a tree(this life one leaf)/ but love is the
sky and i am for you" (25: 367); "Let liars wilt,repaying life they're
loaned;/ we(by a gift called dying born)must grow" (XVI: 398); "love
is a deeper season/ than reason;/ my sweet one/ (and april's where

we're)" (XXXVIII: 412); "only stand with me,love!against these its/ until you are and until i am dreams" (35: 448); "—but never fear(my own,my beautiful/ my blossoming)for also then's until" (69: 466). Such a situation provides Cummings with his most characteristic form for dramatizing his moral ideas.

VII / Additionally, there are smaller groups of poems organized around the statement of a general proposition—"(but born are maids/ to flower an hour/ in all,all)" (23: 365); the expression of an emotion —"i have never loved you dear as now i love" (LI: 259); and the instruction of the reader—"open your heart:/ i'll give you a treasure/ of tiniest world/ a piece of forever" (XLVI: 417).

These, then, are the kinds of responses around which Cummings most characteristically organizes his poems. His five major forms are: the description, that locates its speaker in the presence of some sensory stimulus and represents him as perceiving; praise and eulogy, that place him in relation to some person, type, or idea, and represent him as admiring; the satire, that places him in relation to society and that represents him as its critic; reflection, that places him before scenes and people and represents him as interpreting and commenting; and persuasion, that places him in the presence of someone else and represents him as speaking to him or her. As noted above, there are several additional minor ones which we have not been able to examine in any detail.

A speaker who has over five roles to play simply cannot be characterized as lacking in dramatic and rhetorical range, and thus the usual song-satire distinction will not serve to describe it. Furthermore, a thorough inquiry into Cummings' use of these situations has not supported the contention that he is a static poet, for each of them has an individual history in his work, an origin in time, a rise, and perhaps a fall. There is a decrease in description as he gets older and less absorbed in the immediacy of sensation; a rise, a dip, and a rise in his use of praise and eulogy as he gets a firmer grip on his moral values; a strong current of satire, more and more clearly defining his social values; and a gradual decline in reflection and persuasion as he turns more and more outward toward approbation rather than interpretation, instruction, and consolation. If his growth reveals no crises, it does show a steady development.

A dramatic necessity goes deep into the nature of the sentence. Sentences are not different enough to hold the attention unless they are dramatic. No ingenuity of varying structure will do. All that can save them is the speaking tone of voice somehow entangled in the words and fastened to the page for the ear of the imagination. This is all that can save poetry from sing-song, all that can save prose from itself.

—Robert Frost, Foreword to *A Way Out*

CHAPTER THREE voice

If the poet's vision determines in general the kinds of poems he writes, then it is the kinds of poems he writes that determine the styles he uses.

I / R. P. Blackmur has complained that Cummings' language is frequently unintelligible because he disregards the historical accumulation of meaning inherent in words in favor of merely private and personal associations. But the words a poet puts into the mouth of his persona, and their peculiar combinations, are governed by what he wants us to think and feel about this speaker and what he wants his speaker to accomplish dramatically and rhetorically, whether he is alone and re-flecting, with his lady and persuading, or instructing the reader. He does this by providing us with various clues as to the nature and occasion of the speaker's utterance, while at the same time creating a lin-guistic structure in which one word acts upon another in such a way as to modify and delimit mutually the meanings that it is possible to discover in the poem. The principle here is indeed intelligibility, or appropriateness, or, when liberally interpreted, what used to be called decorum. A certain kind of vocabulary in a certain set of circumstances produces what may be called a tone of voice. Our sense of this tone will be conditioned by what we normally expect to hear in such a situation in relation to what we actually do hear. Mockery, in a serious situation, will result in more than mockery; earnestness, in a comic situation, will be more than earnestness. Intelligibility, then, is an individual matter with each poem and cannot be decided in advance merely by reference to a theory of the history of language.

With Cummings, particularly, this is a complex matter, for nothing is more characteristic of his style than its range and variety. He makes fun of what he praises, and mocks what he reveres; he is seriously funny, comically serious, and classically romantic. He can use obsceni-ties in a love poem and archaisms in a topical satire; he can mix con-crete adjectives with abstract nouns and see colors in terms of sounds. Thus I shall call his general stylistic quality "mixed." Although the mixed style is characteristic of much modern poetry, what is impressive is the particular nature of Cummings' mixture and the special way he handles it.

The components of this mixture—whether appearing alone or in combination—range, reading from right to left on the linguistic spec-trum, from "formal" or "archaic," to "neutral," to "mock" or "bur-lesque." These three modes and their various mixtures constitute an instrument of great dramatic and rhetorical precision which Cummings has forged to characterize the subtlety and variety of his speaker's attitudes and responses. Since there appears to be almost no limit to what his speaker can say in a given situation—he may talk out of the side of his mouth, or sing, or speak grandiloquently, or combine various voices —this verbal freedom is his chief pitfall. But here, as elsewhere, Cummings' freedom transcends danger—or rather lives on danger—and comes out finally as discipline.

I shall take up, to begin with, the characteristics of these components in their relatively "pure" states, and then conclude by examining how Cummings mixes them.

At the center of Cummings' style is a vocabulary of a certain sort, and this is what I have termed his "neutral mode." Briefly, it may be defined as a modified romantic style, which is romantic because of the quality and quantity of certain "sweet," "soft," "warm," and "moist" words, such as *delicious* and *exquisite,* and modified because of the frequent intrusion of antipathetic or "plain," "hard," "cool," and "dry" words, such as *exact* and *stern.* And, because such juxtaposition allows Cummings either to intensify or modify certain traditional associations of certain traditional words, it is this flexible neutral mode that allows him to meet the demands of intelligibility by suiting the history of language, on the one hand, to the needs of the individual poem, on the other.

Taking a hint from the notes of T. E. Hulme and other similar twentieth-century critical writings, we may identify a sweet, soft, warm, and moist vocabulary as that which is traditionally associated with romantic poetry. Its physical qualities are fluidity, mellifluousness, and musicality; its semantic qualities are spirituality, lack of concreteness, and imprecision; and its referents are either subtle or violent inner states. In its extremes it becomes dull, cloudy, and verbose—everything our early twentieth-century poets and critics thought they saw in the Victorians and which they spurned.

A plain, hard, cool, and dry vocabulary, on the other hand, is traditionally associated with "classical" or metaphysical poetry. Its physical qualities are flatness, sharpness, and prosiness; its semantic qualities are materiality, concreteness, and precision; and its referents are personal restraint and social discipline. Its virtues are clarity, wit, and compression, or everything Hulme and others wanted to re-establish in our poetic tradition.

Now let us observe the behavior of these vocabularies as they are combined by Cummings:

one's not half two. It's two are halves of one:
which halves reintegrating,shall occur
no death and any quantity;but than
all numerable mosts the actual more

minds ignorant of stern miraculous
this every truth—beware of heartless them
(given the scalpel,they dissect a kiss;
or,sold the reason,they undream a dream)

one is the song which fiends and angels sing:
all murdering lies by mortals told make two.
Let liars wilt,repaying life they're loaned;
we(by a gift called dying born)must grow

deep in dark least ourselves remembering
love only rides his year.
                    All lose,whole find   (XVI: 398)

Here the speaker warns his lady to avoid those who substitute quantitative for qualitative values, and instructs her in the truths of a love that involves transcendence of the merely temporal and mundane. Surely this is a romantic subject and situation, and the poem is correspondingly replete with such romantic words as "miraculous," "kiss," "dream," "angels," "deep," "dark," and "love." But notice how the vague and subjective are tempered in the direction of the precise and public by the correlative presence of such classical or metaphysical words as "reintegrating," "stern," "dissect," "repaying," "loaned," and "fiends." The point is that such a love as this speaker advocates, although it places lovers beyond good and evil as we know such things in the unworld of materiality, is not easily achieved nor does it come to those who merely relax into a sensual swoon. It is a love achieved only through the discipline of surrender: "All lose,whole find."

These are the values defining the thought and character of the speaker of this poem and this is the situation and the language through which such values are defined. The special quality of this language is the peculiar clash of vocabularies which trims the uncut edges from traditionally romantic words and their chains of association. There is no egoistic self-indulgence here, no wailing after the moon, no private baby-talk babbling of obscure sensations, no willful distortions of language out of pure love of thrills and mischief. Cummings' love may be "miraculous," but it is also "stern." He uses tradition, but in his own unique way; for, although such words as "miraculous" are historically associated with romantic love, and although he uses them quite intelligibly in that same connection, such words as "reintegrate" are not so associated. Thus he merges into one co-operative adventure the demands of the language and the needs of the poem.

If there is any obscurity in this poem, it is easily dissolved once the reader understands Cummings' habit of transforming other parts of speech into nouns. Such a grammatical shift alters the forms but not the meanings of words: "but than/ all numerable mosts the actual more" is simply a distinctive way of saying that love's quality has comparatively more value than any superlative quantity.

This clash of vocabularies is the central fact of Cummings' style with which we must come to grips if we are to understand his use of language. We may say that this style originates in what he calls "carnalized metaphysics; or, abstractions raised to the power of the concrete" (quoted from a letter to the present writer, referring to the devices of personification). His vision of life, although transcendental, begins in an early and never-failing sensuous delight in the physical world, both urban and rural. It is the social world, the world of manmade anxieties and routines, that he transcends and not, as is sometimes believed, the physical or cultural worlds. Not death but the fear of death is what he scorns, and not the living cultural tradition but the sterile convention.

His adjectives, of which there are a large number and variety indeed, are equally cosmic and material, vague and specific, ideal and real, referring as often to concepts as to physical qualities. "Immortal," "illimitable," and "unimaginable" are just as characteristic as "silent," "bright," and "thick." For Cummings, the natural world pulsates at certain moments with a supernatural vibrancy, and these moments are at once the symbols of and the gateway to the transcendent world. In this manner the sensationalist becomes the mystic, and this is the language that results.

There is a similar combination of abstract and concrete in his choice of nouns. Cummings is a poet with a serious vision of life, rather than the anti-intellectual sensationalist he is still being taken for. What is especially characteristic, regarding his use of abstract nouns, is his wholesale transformation of other parts of speech into nouns. These are often paired to denote conceptual opposites or contrasts, for Cummings' world, as we know by now, is divided into a heaven—the dream world of faith and fulfillment—and a hell—the unworld of fear and automatism—which together form the basis for an intelligible and philosophical set of moral values. Thus the meanings embodied in such words as "now" *vs.* "never" or "here" *vs.* "where," although coming to us with a unique and personal flavor as the result of a grammatical shift, are nevertheless perfectly comprehensible as expressions of the philosophy of life that Cummings espouses, which is transcendental, romantic, prelapsarian, organicist, and individualistic. The same is publicly available in the writings of many others, such as Emerson, Whitman, Thoreau, and Emily Dickinson. We may wish to take issue with such a view but we cannot attack it as obscure.

Regarding Cummings' more conventionally handled abstract nouns, which refer, sometimes metonymically, to man's faculties and their products, we may note that "dream," particularly, epitomizes his concept of the transcendental world. "Memory" is the common avenue down which the reflecting and observing persona walks, and "heart" and "soul," though often set in romantic opposition to "mind," are not always merely the favored pair, since he frequently ridicules his automatons for lacking mind as well:

he does not have to feel because he thinks
(the thoughts of others,be it understood)
he does not have to think because he knows
(that anything is bad which you think good)   (23: 292)

    *

when Souls are outlawed,Hearts are sick,
Hearts being sick,Minds nothing can   (54: 314)

    *

Without a heart the animal
is very very kind
so kind it wouldn't like a soul
and couldn't use a mind   (IV: 391)

Or again, such cosmic nouns as "mystery," "doom," and "splendor" represent attempts at expressing the inexpressable and are essential parts of the mystic's vocabulary for describing the ineffable and transcendent sphere of spiritual fulfillment central to Cummings' conceptual world. So, too, are words denoting emotions such as "hope," "fear," and "ecstasy." These appear often in pairs, either by way of contrast or by way of encompassing fearlessly a set of extremes. Nouns referring to qualities are used either synaesthetically or to denote abstractions: we encounter in Cummings' poetry the "colors" of a smile, the "gesture" of a brain, the "music" of a sunset, or the "silence" of a voice rather more frequently than in the verse of other poets.

Although he writes many descriptive poems, Cummings was never an imagist; nor does he make a fetish of avoiding adjectives. Neither is he wary of adverbs, of which by far the largest number denotes manner. Whether dealing with perceptual movement, mental or emotional movement, an abstract-concrete mixture of the two, or a paradoxical combination of opposites, his continuing concern with the way in which things happen or are done is reflected by such words as "gently," "cleverly," and "spontaneously," which partially accounts for the strong effect of motion one gets as he reads the poetry. Adverbs denoting degree mirror a concern with quantity, which is also a strong characteristic of Cummings' language. Such adverbs give an impression of definiteness mixed with a tentative quality, which produces a hovering, paradoxical, and delicate effect, as in "wholly and probably" or "impossibly and utterly." This seems entirely appropriate in view of his sensationalist-transcendentalist values. Adverbs of speed such as "abruptly" and "gradually" confirm the sense of motion noted above, as do those of physical quality such as "silently" and "crisply." Words denoting sound, taste, touch, and sight are fairly prominent, while words denoting smell seem uncommon. The mystic's vocabulary is augmented by adverbs of time, which usually denote timelessness, such as "continually" and "perpetually."

Regarding the matter of growth and decline, the gradual disappearance of such words as "frailly," "utterly," delicately," and "sweetly" indicates a certain amount of pruning, of cutting down on some of the more flagrantly saccharine romantic elements. Nor can we lament the disappearance of such nouns as "sweetness," "fragility," "rapture," and "ecstasy," or of such adjectives as "fragile," "frail," "pale," "golden," "slim," and "smooth." As in other aspects of Cummings' art and thought, there has been, if not a sudden change, a gradual tightening of his style.

His chief distinction in the use of verbs is a penchant for clusters of homophonic words denoting either sound or movement—"swoop," "hurl," "wriggle," "twitch." The cumulative effect of the frequent use of such words, expressing as they do violence of motion and gesture and sound, is one of distortion and stress, especially since they are often used either synaesthetically in connection with nonhuman phenomena to produce an impression of vivid and even startling personification—as when a sunset "chatters," for example—or in connection with people and human actions to produce an impression of disgust, comedy, pity, horror, and outrage—as when a girl's sex "squeaks" like a billiard cue. Most of these verbs serve to counterbalance the softness already noted as characteristic of a large portion of his vocabulary.

Cummings' neutral vocabulary, regarded as a whole, then, is not any one thing. Although such words as "bright," "mystery," "wholly," and "float" loom large, there are an almost equal number of such words as "brittle," "brain," "abruptly," and "bang" to produce a contrapuntal effect. This juxtaposition and strain mark his neutral style, so that the speaker's tone is rarely entirely serious or sarcastic or joking or reverential in any one poem but is rather, even when most "neutral," shifting and changing:

    whose are these(wraith a clinging with a wraith)

    ghosts drowning in supreme thunder?ours
    (over you reels and me a moon;beneath,

    bombed the by ocean earth bigly shudders)

    never was death so alive:chaos so(hark
    —that screech of space)absolute(my soul
    tastes If as some world of a spark

    's gulped by illimitable hell)

    and never have breathed such miracle murdered we
    whom cannot kill more mostful to arrive
    each(futuring snowily which sprints for the
    crumb of our Now)twiceuponatime wave—

    put out your eyes,and touch the black skin
    of an angel named imagination   (41: 451–52)

This is a poem of persuasion in which the speaker is represented as instructing his lady in the symbolic values of the booming of the surf below and the glowing of the moon overhead at night, emblems of Death and Time, and of the dream world, respectively. He tells her that, by virtue of the power of the creative imagination (moon) and although apparently swallowed up and destroyed by the encroaching waves, they transcend the powers of Death and Time and become immortal because they are there in experience "now" and surrendering to it. Notice the occurrence of such characteristically soft words as "wraith," "supreme," "shudders," "illimitable," "miracle," and "imagination," as well as that of such typically hard words as "bombed," "screech," "gulped," and "sprints." This poem exemplifies a relatively "pure" instance of Cummings' neutral style, while at the same time embodying a relatively serious tone and situation. It is clear that this language is called into being by the peculiar dramatic necessities of the situation informing this poem as well as by the general qualities of Cummings' vision. The speaker, as usual, talks in the character of an artist, and is thus concerned with both the concreteness of the scene and with its meaning; his lady is both an object of devotion calling forth his comments and a person of deep perception sharing his moment of transcendence; and the doctrine he expounds to her, being based upon the paradox of victory through surrender, and combining as it does the clash of opposites (alive death, absolute chaos, screech of space, breathe-miracle-murdered-kill, and so on), requires naturally the use of so flexible and various a stylistic instrument.

Also exemplified here is a characteristic phraseology which marks Cummings' style throughout, especially in his last three volumes: "more mostful to arrive each." Such comparative and superlative adjectives as "least," "most," and "more," "less," and such pronouns of quantity as "each," "all," "every," "some," "any," "only," "merely," and "much" (frequently related or compounded with such pronouns of time, number, and space, as "when," "thing," and "where"), and the various combinations thereof, account for an effect of constant choosing, preferring, discriminating, of overtopping the best and the worst, and of the transcendence of extremes. In the poem cited above, for example, the phrase in question modifies "wave," and the implication is that, although *each* wave batters the shore with *more* than ut*most* violence, froths impetuously, is succeeded by the next wave, and grasps for the fixed present of the lovers in an effort to undermine it by the moving flux of the future, the lovers will survive such a threat through the office of the poetic imagination.

The effect is frequently one of conceptual intensification, as in "his least unmotion roams the youngest star" (11: 435), or in "more much than all" and "one small/ most of a rose" (10: 434), or in "swim so now million many worlds in each/ least less than particle of perfect dark"

(5: 431), where the smallest or the largest becomes even smaller or larger to emphasize Cummings' transcendentalism. Such intensification becomes, ultimately, the mutual blending of extremes wherein the lesser absorbs the greater, which is one chief kind of paradox or reconciliation of opposites that Cummings practices:

life is more true than reason will deceive
(more secret or than madness did reveal)
deeper is life than lose:higher than have
—but beauty is more each than living's all

    .   .   .   .   .

(here less than nothing's more than everything)

death,as men call him,ends what they call men
—but beauty is more now than dying's when   (LII: 421)

An exact illustration of how to say "beauty outlasts the grave" in a fresh and original manner, this poem exemplifies, as well, Cummings' habit of reversing what are to him the inverted values of most people by means of a characteristically individual way of phrasing comparatives and superlatives.

II / Varying to the right of this norm produces a purely serious, archaic, reverential, and formal style, while varying to the left creates a purely vulgar, violent, burlesque, and mock style; and, it is clear, each of these extremes has its special utility for glorifying and ridiculing, respectively. Since praise and satire are two of Cummings' most commonly used forms, accounting between them for at least 40 per cent of his work as a whole, we are likely to meet each of these extremes frequently.

Cummings has shown greater interest in the burlesque than in the archaic style. Although the latter plays a large part in his first volume, *Tulips and Chimneys* (1922), he used it much more sparingly in all his subsequent volumes. Perhaps this is because *Tulips and Chim-*

neys is chiefly "literary" and derivative, but the fact remains that he will still use such a style when the occasion arises. And which of our modern poets has dared to be so reactionary? Most poets writing today would feel embarrassed to use the archaic style seriously, yet Cummings does it:

> we thank thee
> god
> almighty for dying
>
> (forgive us,o life!the sin of Death   (6: 432)

Take the softer elements of Cummings' neutral mode, and combine them with outmoded forms, such as "thou," "thy," "hath," and you have his most serious formal style, of which the following is an early example:

> Thy fingers make early flowers of
> all things.
> thy hair mostly the hours love:
> a smoothness which
> sings, saying
> (though love be a day)
> do not fear, we will go amaying.   (III: 11)

And here is a late example:

> what of the wonder
> (beingest growingest)
> over all under
> all hate all fear
> —all perfectly dyingest
> my and foreverless
> thy?
>   why our
> is love and neverless   (L: 420)

There is a distinction to be made between late and early archaic, largely on the basis of the developing recurrence of his conceptual idiom. Such words as "beingest," "growingest," "over," "under," "dyingest," "foreverless," and "neverless" give the latter poem a maturity and a weight of personal conviction that are almost entirely absent from the former poem because it is so much more secondhand.

The former poem was grouped as a "Song" in *Tulips and Chimneys,* and an Elizabethan melodiousness, a quality that Cummings has always excelled in producing, even more in his later work than in his youth, is an effect of his poetry that we would do well to examine as an aspect of his formal style. For archaisms, tending as they do to suit praise and glorification and a reverential and prayerful tone, and so frequently associated with art-song and hymn, carry with them an aura of melody that is intensified by their resemblance to sixteenth- and seventeenth-century poetry which was often written for or set to music. Many of Cummings' poems have actually been given a musical setting and performed publicly at concerts. Furthermore, the poem of praise also tends to create an effect of song, and this is a form that Cummings shares with the Elizabethans and that he handles more frequently than most modern poets, many of whom are cultivating a deliberately prosaic style. Then, too, Cummings frequently organizes the sequence of his poems on a repetitive and parallelistic basis, a trait that reflects the influence of such lyrics as Campion's "Cherry-Ripe" and Carew's "Ask Me No More," both, incidentally, poems of praise. Take for example the following, which is also a poem of praise:

> if everything happens that can't be done
> (and anything's righter
> than books
> could plan)
> the stupidest teacher will almost guess
> (with a run
> skip
> around we go yes)
> there's nothing as something as one
>
> one hasn't a why or because or although
> (and buds know better

than books
don't grow)
one's anything old being everything new
(with a what
which
around we come who)
one's everyanything so

so world is a leaf so tree is a bough
(and birds sing sweeter
than books
tell how)
so here is away and so your is a my
(with a down
up
around again fly)
forever was never till now

now i love you and you love me
(and books are shuter
than books
can be)
and deep in the high that does nothing but fall
(with a shout
each
around we go all)
there's somebody calling who's we

we're anything brighter than even the sun
(we're everything greater
than books
might mean)
we're everyanything more than believe
(with a spin
leap
alive we're alive)
we're wonderful one times one   (LIV: 422–23)

Here every stanza not only matches every other as far as the disposition of stresses, line lengths, and rhymes is concerned, but also in terms of the way in which each phrase or syntactical unit of each stanza is balanced by a similar phrase or unit in a similar position in every other stanza. This device in written and spoken poetry is analogous to the way in which each separate verse of a song is sung to the same melody and tends to produce, therefore, a similar "lyrical" effect. Cummings' essays are also often characterized by an elaborately balanced prose style. Combine, then, a purity of formal tone and style with a joyful subject, such as the celebration of love, and a delicately varying yet strictly sustained system of repetition and balance, and you have a poetic song, a "lyric" in the true sense of the word. It is this type of poem that, to my mind, represents one of Cummings' major contributions to modern English and American poetry.

III / Cummings' burlesque style, at the other extreme, is more virile —a different matter entirely. If he is unashamed of being openly reverential, he is equally unhesitant about being downright sarcastic. His burlesque style is a rich mixture of elements, of which the commentators have discussed only his New Yorkese vulgarisms. Some have been embarrassed by this aspect of Cummings' style, and have decided that it is Park Avenue trying to talk like the Bowery, "slumming in morals along with he-men and lady social workers." But there is much more to it than that.

The New Yorkese element did not enter his work until *is 5* (1926):

> . . . "I'll tell duh woild; some noive all right.
> Aint much on looks but how dat baby ached." (II: 165)

This, it is essential to remember, is "Mame" speaking, a whore who has just returned from having her tooth pulled; and a reading of the whole poem reveals that its speaker or narrator (Mame's visitor) uses standard English:

she puts down the handmirror. "Look at" arranging
before me a mellifluous idiot grin

Cummings is interested in giving a dramatic impression of one of the
creatures of his demimonde by allowing her to speak in her own language. The effect is one of comic pathos, achieved in the contrast between the bravado of the diction on the one hand and the wretched circumstances of the character on the other. A similar effect is found in
another poem:

oil tel duh woil doi sez
dooyuh unnurs tanmih eesez pullih nizmus tash,oi
dough un giv uh shid oi sez.   Tom
oidoughwuntuh doot,butoiguttuh
braikyooz,datswut eesez tuhmih. . . .   (II: 224)

A more comically ludicrous effect is produced, however, in the following:

in dem daze kid Christmas
meant sumpn youse knows wot
i refers ter Satter Nailyuh . . .   (VIII: 172)

Or in this sample:

buncha hardboil guys frum duh A.C. fulla
hooch kiddin eachudder bout duh clap an
talkin big how dey could kill
sixereight cops— . . .   (XXIII: 239)

We see that it all depends upon who is talking and what he is saying.
So far such phonetically spelled gutter-talk has been used either to
arouse pity or laughter, or both. But there are more serious uses, as in
the Hemingway satire (26: 294) or in "ygUDuh" (VII: 393), where
ridicule and hatred are aroused by the use of New Yorkese. In rare instances the persona himself speaks that way, as in the following where
he describes distastefully the efforts of modern parents to disabuse their
children of the "psychotic myth" of Santa Claus, and then turns to all

real people, "all joybegotten whelps," who still believe in such myths, "like Jonah And The Whale," and says:

> :oiwun uhsoi roitee runow dutmoi
> jak roids wid yooze
> Vury Sin Silly
> :oi   (15: 288)

Much of this diction resembles the speech of Herriman's Krazy Kat; as we know, Cummings wrote an introduction to a collection of that cartoonist's work. This argot permits the formation of various comic puns, like "Sin Silly," for example. The whole statement can be transliterated as "I want to say right here and now that my jack rides with you—Very Sincerely, I." If the people and attitudes he is satirizing are proper and *au courant,* he emphasizes the distinction between them and others like himself who are more old-fashioned by speaking the language of the gutter modified by the locutions of a love-crazy cat of ambiguous gender who speaks like a gentle New York Jewish fruit peddler.

Since *is 5* (1926) Cummings has tended to use New Yorkese less frequently, but he has continued the device of phonetic rendering of other dialects, even in his latest work:

> He
>   no
>   care
>   so
>   what
> yoo-gointa-doo? . . .   (20: 440)

or

> hooz
> gwine ter
> hate
> dad hurt
> fool wurl no gal no
> boy
>   (day simbully loves id) . . .   (33: 373)

And in these cases it is crucial to note that both speakers, a foreign-born ice-coal-wood man and a Negro guitarist, are presented through the medium of their own speech as specimens of decent, if humble, human beings.

Colloquialisms, of the kind used in this early Buffalo Bill poem, have always been a part of Cummings' style:

> Jesus
>
> he was a handsome man
>   and what i want to know is
> how do you like your blueeyed boy
> Mister Death   (VIII: 50)

This late World War II poem is similar:

> can't you see now no not
> any christ but you
> must understand
> why because
> i am
> dead   (40: 451)

The conversational voice, almost as characteristic of Cummings as the singing voice, may be used by his own persona, as in the first example cited above, or by some other speaker entirely, as in the second example.

Nor are slang expressions and vulgarities alien to such an informal tone: "abslatively posolutely dead" (III: 59); "wouldn't that/ get yer goat" (V: 88); "she got the info/ from a broad that knew Eddie in Topeka" (XVI: 113); "waiting for the bulls to pull his joint" (XX: 114); "both all hopped/ up" (IX: 229). Rough diction has always been considered as decorum for satirical poems, even by the strictest of classical critics; and it is largely for the purposes of comedy and ridicule that Cummings has either his own persona or other assorted speakers talk in this way.

Although he has not gone so far as to print, without distorting their normal spelling (cf. IV: 86–87; II: 224; XXX: 244; and 54: 314), the familiar four-letter words referring to digestive and sexual functions, he is not above using an occasional obscenity in an appropriate place, or even building an entire poem around one, as in:

> the way to hump a cow is not
> to get yourself a stool
> but draw a line around the spot
> and call it beautifool   (14: 359)

This poem is spoken by an old-time political hack telling an aspirant the secrets of successful electioneering, and the fruits of wisdom he has garnered from experience are cynical—

> to vote for me(all decent mem
> and wonens will allows
> which if they don't to hell with them)
> is hows to hump a cows   (14: 360)

Such a style seems to me entirely appropriate to a situation involving such a hateful person. The poem is perhaps even more complicated by the fact that the satire hovers ambiguously between attacking the gullible electorate, on the one hand, and the cynical politician who *thinks* they are gullible, on the other. The target is the politician *and* those who *are* gullible, for it is clear from the last stanza quoted above, first, that it is a politician who speaks, and second, that some voters do not fall for his line.

A fifth element of Cummings' burlesque style, the obverse of the use of New Yorkese and vulgarisms, is constituted of the mock-archaic, mock-formal or Latinate language, periphrases, and hyperbolic prefixes. Cummings frequently uses high-flown language ironically and sarcastically with devastating effect: "yonder deadfromtheneckup graduate" (V: 170); "wherefore yon mob" (XVI: 176); "One wondrous fine sonofabitch" (XXV: 181); "a dozen staunch and leal/ citizens" (XXVIII: 184); "ponder,darling,these busted statues/ of yon motheaten forum" (XXX: 186); "the season 'tis, my lovely lambs" (I: 191); "yon clean upstanding well dressed boy" (VIII: 195); " 'Gay' is the captivating cognomen of a Young Woman" (XVIII: 236); "!ye/ galleon/ wilts" (6: 282); "o pr/ gress verily thou art m/ mentous superc/ lossal/ hyperpr/ digious" (9: 284); "Life,dost Thou contain a marvel than/ this death named Smith less strange?" (23: 293); "ye twang of little joe(yankee)gould irketh sundry" (27: 294); "all history oped her teeming womb" (XII: 395); "the/ great pink/ superme/ diocri/ ty of/ a hyperhypocritical D/ mocra/ c" (37: 449–50). These examples show the opposite side of the coin of his true archaic and formal style, and illustrate perfectly the wide range of his speaking voice.

A sixth and somewhat similar stylistic device is the parody, mock-literary allusion, or comical pun. In the second chapter I have remarked upon the ways in which Browning, Kipling, Longfellow, and other great poets are pressed into service, and may now note, in addition, Cummings' continuing habit of burlesquing patriotic songs and slogans, advertising claims, and political clichés:

> take it from me kiddo
> believe me
> my country, 'tis of
>
> you, land of the Cluett
> Shirt Boston Garter and Spearmint
> Girl With The Wrigley Eyes(of you
> land of the Arrow Ide
> and Earl &
> Wilson
> Collars) of you i
> sing:land of Abraham Lincoln and Lydia E. Pinkham,
> land above all of Just Add Hot Water And Serve—
> from every B. V. D.
>
> let freedom ring
>
> amen. . . .   (II: 167)

This is a satire of the dead language that symbolizes a dead culture in general and patriotic, commercial, and artistic clichés in particular; and the technique consists in repeating, with slight twists, in the context of the persona's own angry voice ("i do however protest," "i would/ suggest"), the actual words and phrases that typify the linguistic abuse that is itself under attack. This is an early, well-known example; the following illustrates a later and somewhat different use of parody:

> red-rag and pink-flag
> blackshirt and brown
> strut-mince and stink-brag
> have all come to town
>
> some like it shot
> and some like it hung
> and some like it in the twot
> nine months young   (II: 357–58)

Not only do we find some startling vulgarisms here, but we also notice how the deadly effect of this satire on Communism-Fascism-Nazism is intensified tenfold by the clearly recognizable allusions to the nursery rhymes, "Hark, Hark, the Dogs Do Bark" in the first stanza and "Pease Porridge Hot" in the second. Whereas in the first poem cited Cummings used the very language of those he would lampoon, in this one he alludes to an opposite sort of thing altogether—a world of joy and innocence—from what he would satirize—a world of hate and misery— thereby emphasizing the effect by a subtle contrast rather than by exaggeration and the *reductio ad absurdum* method. Cummings is also frequently fond of punning on the names of famous people—"Robinson Jefferson," "Injustice Taughed," "Wouldwoe Washington" (XIII: 232–33); "Amy Sandburg," "Algernon Carl Swinburned" (IV: 170)— as well as official titles—"THE UNCOMMONWEALTH OF HUMANUSETTS" (XVII: 236)—and reversed homonyms—"wrongers who write what they are dine to live" (XXVI: 242).

IV / The three styles described so far have been theoretically pure types—neutral, formal, and burlesque; but there is a fourth mode which exists anywhere along the spectrum from one extreme, through neutral, to the other; and this I have called "mixed." Nowhere is Cummings' versatility so clearly in evidence as in his many poems containing a compound of voices and tones. Even his neutral mode, as we have seen, is "neutral" only in his special manner.

Let us bracket our target by citing an early poem illustrating this style, and then a late one:

death is more than
certain a hundred these
sounds crowds odours it
is in a hurry
beyond that any this
taxi smile or angle we do

not sell and buy
things so necessary as
is death and unlike shirts
neckties trousers
we cannot wear it out

no sir which is why
granted who discovered
America ether the movies
may claim general importance

to me to you nothing is
what particularly
matters hence in a

little sunlight and less
moonlight ourselves against the worms

hate laugh shimmy   (IX: 172–73)

Notice the mixture of voices and the shifts in tone: the first two stanzas are serious enough in tone and neutral enough in style, except for the gradually developing effect of incongruity that results from his peculiar choice of analogies—for example, "death is more in a hurry than any taxi." Beginning with the third stanza the speaker begins to slip into a colloquial and mock-formal style—"no sir which is why," "granted . . . may claim general importance." Somewhere between the fourth and fifth stanzas his tone becomes most serious—"sunlight," "moonlight," "worms"; and at the end, with the progression "hate laugh shimmy," he engages in one final reversal back to a colloquial and vulgar tone. And why? Surely his subject is serious, the most serious a poet can choose. The speaker is stating a proposition: Death is certain, in a hurry, necessary, durable, and important; therefore we, as opposed to the citizens of the unworld who pin their faith upon transitory things, live out our lives against the permanent backdrop of a belief in death. He is talking to people of imagination, then, and uses a neutral, a colloquial, and then a vulgar tone by way of emphasizing the increasing seriousness of his meaning, by contrast and by way of symbolizing a humorous readiness to believe in the reality of death. For the speaker and his audience are not frightened by such a thought.

Consider the following as a late example of the mixed mode:

no time ago
or else a life
walking in the dark
i met christ

jesus)my heart
flopped over
and lay still
while he passed(as

close as i'm to you
yes closer
made of nothing
except loneliness   (50: 455)

Again a very serious subject, and again the speaker's tone modulates through several variations. He opens seriously, except for the slight and delicate hint of a fairy-tale beginning (compare "anyone lived in a pretty how town," 29: 370–71)—"no time ago" suggests "a long time

ago there lived . . . ." The tone becomes even more serious in the
second line because of the allusion in the first—"or else a life." The first
half of the second stanza, because of the way in which Christ's name
is spaced, opens colloquially—"jesus! my heart," and continues in the
same manner with "flopped over." The second half of the second stanza
is neutral enough; and the pattern is repeated once again in the third and
last stanza—colloquial in "close as i'm to you/ yes closer"—and neutral
in "made of nothing/ except loneliness." The speaker narrates an emotional experience he had, and the whole effect is of an intensely serious,
yet naively personal and humble, reaction to a vision of God's presence
on earth. By means of such a delicately responsive stylistic instrument,
Cummings naturally avoids pomposity and inflated holiness. His treatment of Christianity is Unitarian, as the following Christmas poem
amply demonstrates:

> (and i imagine
> never mind Joe agreeably cheerfully remarked when
> surrounded by fat stupid animals
> the jewess shrieked
> the messiah tumbled successfully into the world
> the animals continued eating.   And i imagine she, and
> heard them slobber and
> in the darkness)
>
> stood sharp angels with faces like Jim Europe   (XII: 174)

If the meanings of poetic language emerge from a co-operative inter-
play between the demands of linguistic history and the needs of the
individual poem, and if Cummings' poetic language is built upon such
dramatic interaction, then it may be claimed that his poetry, far from
being obscure, is public and intelligible while at the same time unique
and individual. Cummings' poetry, in stemming from a complex but
comprehensible sensationalist-transcendentalist philosophy of life, makes
use of a mixture of the sweet and the plain styles, which modifies their
historical associations to suit the needs of a special poetic temperament
as well as the formal demands of any given poetic context.

I do not conclude, however, that a poet can make anything he wants out of language, but rather that he can select, from out of the variety of meanings with which historical association has clothed a word, those that he deems suitable to the dramatic needs of his poem. Thus we have examined as the chief general characteristic of Cummings' style the ways in which his use of romantic words is modified and limited in certain dramatic contexts by a strong influx of unromantic words, even of vulgarisms, with the result that the traditional vocabulary, while retaining its historical character, will never be quite the same again. And that sort of linguistic transformation is a true poet's work.

The perfection of Diction is for it to be at once clear and not mean. The clearest indeed is that made up of the ordinary words for things, but it is mean. . . . A certain admixture, accordingly, of unfamiliar terms is necessary. These, the strange word, the metaphor, the ornamental equivalent, etc., will save the language from seeming mean and prosaic, while the ordinary words in it will secure the requisite clearness. What helps most, however, to render the Diction at once clear and non-prosaic is the use of the lengthened, curtailed, and altered forms of words. Their deviation from the ordinary words will, by making the language unlike that in general use, give it a non-prosaic appearance; and their having much in common with the words in general use will give it the quality of clearness. It is not right, then, to condemn these modes of speech, and ridicule the poet for using them, as some have done. . . . It is a great thing, indeed, to make a proper use of these poetical forms, as also of compounds and strange words.

—Aristotle, *Poetics* 1458^{a}18–1459^{a}5, ch. 22 (Bywater translation)

CHAPTER FOUR device

The general functions of the devices and techniques of the poetic art are to render what is being shown as intelligible and yet as vivid as possible. There is, fortunately or unfortunately, no general principle as to the proper relationship between these two functions. Sometimes they are at odds—when too much clarity flattens the impact, or too much impact obscures the clarity—and the poet has to strike a compromise; but ideally they co-operate—when just enough information is presented

86

in such a way as to insure the maximum imaginative effect upon the reader.

Technically, the poet's job is to fashion this ideal co-operation for each poem, and he may do this either by using the accepted tools of his tradition or by fashioning new ones. He who chooses the latter path is an experimentalist—even though all good poets working within the tradition make the usual techniques do new things—because he re-works the accepted devices beyond recognition or even invents new ones never used before. Nor is he to be valued any the more or less because of that. With traditionalist or experimentalist alike the question is not how far or near he has gotten in relation to the tradition, but rather how well his device, new or old, has done what he intends it to do. The chief difference is that the experimentalist is harder to analyze because critical terms and concepts to describe his work are lacking.

Cummings is in this sense an experimental poet. Although his subjects, ideas, and situations are frequently ultra-traditional because they resemble more the poetry of Campion than of Wallace Stevens, his techniques and devices are frequently ultra-modern because he has taken a completely individual attitude toward rhyme, meter, stanza, grammar, syntax, and typography. In these matters he has either extended old devices beyond their usual function or has made new devices altogether.

Exactly how and why he does this is a matter for detailed analysis, but at the outset it will be useful to set up a few general terms. Intelligibility and vividness involve, among other things, what the language of a poem expresses and how the handling of language intensifies the imaginative impact of the expression. Any given device, therefore, may serve to put before us a clearer notion of what is being expressed, whether an object, action, feeling, or concept; or to make what is being expressed more moving by means of emphasis, sound, rhythm, or suggestion. These conceptual and aesthetic effects are usually found in combination but are more easily studied as if they were separate.

The ways in which any poet manages to produce these effects are, generally speaking, to supply analogies through figures of speech; to arrange organizational units through rhyme, meter, and stanza, in terms of which he can deploy his material for the sake of variety in regularity; to produce intensity through manipulating grammatical and syntactical units; or to create emphasis through repetition or suspense, augmentation or subtraction, statement or implication. What Cummings adds to the usual devices includes word-coinage, the shifting of grammatical forms, syntactical and typographical dislocation, and blending stanzaic patterns with free verse.

What follows is a discussion of the growth and development of these several devices in Cummings' poetry regarding their various effects, proceeding from the least to the most experimental. We shall begin with an analysis of his figurative language which, although handled in a characteristic manner, is his most traditionally used device. We shall then examine in turn his metrical and stanzaic practices, his habits of word-coinage and syntactical distortion, and finally his use of typographical units for poetic purposes.

I / Cummings' earlier poetry is marked by a density of vivid figurative effects:

> the sky a silver
> dissonance by the correct
> fingers of April
> resolved
>
>   into a
> clutter of trite jewels
>
> now like a moth with stumbling
>
> wings flutters and flops along the
> grass collides with trees and
> houses and finally,
> butts into the river   (I: 40)

This is a description of an April shower followed by mist, the expression of which involves at least four figures of speech: (1) synaesthesia

—combining effects of color and sound, as in "silver dissonance"; (2) personification of a season, as in "fingers of April"; (3) metaphor, as in describing raindrops as "a clutter of trite jewels"; and (4) simile, as in mist likened to "a moth with stumbling wings."

Cummings' later poetry, however, depends for its vividness more upon symbol, allegory, paradox, word-coinage, and typographical spacing, than upon such figures. Although there are many striking metaphors and similes in his earlier work—"the/ moon rattles like a fragment of angry candy" (I: 58), or "her tiniest whispered invitation/ is like a clock striking in a dark house" (V: 167) are commonly cited examples —these are not a dominant characteristic of his mature style, as they are, say, of Shakespeare's, Donne's, Keats's, or Meredith's style.

It is as if the functions of metaphor and simile have been taken over by other devices. Cummings moves either from scene to symbol through concept, or from idea to image through allegory; rarely does he seek comparisons between image and idea by importing analogies from outside the poem. In his mature practice he achieves thereby the vividness of dramatic imagery on the one hand, and the clarity and consistency of idea on the other. His later poetry is frequently more lucid, more moving, and more profound than his earlier, and one of the causes of this development regarding his particular style is this shift from simile to symbol.

Take, for example, the following stanza from a later poem celebrating a Greenwich Village scissors-grinder:

> he sharpens is to am
> he sharpens say to sing
> you'd almost cut your thumb
> so right he sharpens wrong   (26: 443)

This scissors-grinder has a marvelous effect upon people as he plies his trade through the city streets, and Cummings expresses that effect, appropriately enough, in terms of sharpening. This expression of one thing in terms of another creates, of course, a figure; but, since the analogy—sharpening equals making people happy—derives from the

literal dramatic situation itself, it is a symbolic rather than a metaphorical figure. That is to say, he is talking about a literal scissors-
grinder as well as the scissors-grinder as a symbol (associated, to be
sure, with the transition from sunset to twilight to evening, which is in
itself a symbol of dreams, imagination, fulfillment, and happiness—
"reminding with his bell/ to disappear a sun/ . . . / to reappear a
moon").

If, then, the analogy exists either as a subject or a pseudo subject in
its own right (as is the city of Byzantium for Yeats), it is symbolic. In
a metaphor, on the other hand, subject and analogy, the latter being
imported from outside the poem, exist as separate entities. Such is the
case in Keats's "Thou still unravish'd bride of quietness": the urn is
literally silent, but it is a "bride" only by virtue of exterior analogy (it
is linked in sterile union with the silence of an early and mysterious
past, as a woman might be married to a man who has as yet refused
to consummate their marriage).

Furthermore, to coin nouns from verbs as Cummings does in this
stanza, a practice which we have already touched upon in other connections and shall have occasion to examine in greater detail below,
gives an additional vividness in that such nouns stand for conceptual
equivalents: "is to am" means that people are transformed by means of
the scissors-grinder's individuality from third-person automatons to first-
person individuals; "say to sing" means that these people, once so
transformed, exist in the dream world of poetry rather than the unworld of prose.

Given, then, a character such as we have described in the first chapter, having certain peculiar values and interests, there is bound to arise
from out of this interaction between scene and concept a set of symbols
or a group of favored images which, by virtue of their recurrence and
the emphasis placed upon them, have become the vehicles of some of
his strongest feelings and attitudes. Most of them are, significantly
enough, derived from nature or are associated in one way or another
with the dream world of fulfillment. Since they recur frequently to-

gether, they form something of a cluster, which perhaps can best be illustrated by the following synthetic situation:

It would be a spring sunset and there would be a mountain or a hill in the middle distance, and a tree nearby with a bird singing in its branches; flowers would be present and the heave and toss of the sea might be heard beyond; then gradually twilight would deepen, a slip of a new moon would appear, and, as night descended, the bright points of starlight would prick the sky; perhaps it might even rain and the entire scene would be darkly dazzled and smoothly hushed by its reflections.

How the speaker might be responding to this scene we have already discussed in the second chapter; here we see his chief symbolic objects: sunset-twilight-night, spring, mountain-ocean, tree-flower-bird, moon-star, and rain. The interesting thing about this symbolism is its simplicity, its absolutely traditional quality; if Cummings' techniques are frequently complex and his subjects often bizarre, his thought and his symbolic imagery are just the reverse. Here we find no old myths revived to provide a framework for the thought of a poet who is trying to synthesize a modern industrial world with a medieval feudal religion; no quests, no voyages, no descents, no fiery wheels, no deaths of vegetation gods, no fisher kings, no waste lands, no symbolic hunting, no allegorical fishing—just a bird in a tree, a mountain in twilight, a new moon, and spring rain.

Out of such commonplace materials, however, Cummings creates his speaker's symbolic world of imagination and possibility, of dreams and miracles, of love and surrender and triumph. Since it is an imagery of transition and transformation, its distinguishing characteristic is its dynamic quality; sunset becoming twilight; twilight becoming night; a moon waxing or waning; a star appearing and disappearing; winter becoming spring; an ocean ebbing and flowing; a tree putting on or taking off its leaves; flowers growing and decaying; a bird darting across the sky; a mountain changing with the seasons; or the arrival and departure of a rain or a snow storm. These elements constitute a world of changes and shifts; they also, existing at night as they do, symbolize a world of hushed, muted, and softened transformation, for dreams are the natural children of night, and love is most often associated with darkness. Nor does the speaker sleep, but lives most intensely at this time and among these things. It is no wonder, then, that as a stylist Cummings makes a point of distinguishing between a noun or a past participle ("death," "made") and the present participle ("dying," "making"), since the latter refers to processes while the former designate fixities.

It remains now to illustrate, choosing those poems most clearly focused on each of these symbols. The poem on a star cited in the first chapter, "morsel miraculous and meaningless," for example, is one of several devoted exclusively to that symbol, which, as we have seen, represents the pulsation of life beyond time. The flower, most frequently noted as Cummings' favorite image, is chiefly an erotic symbol, standing for the lady's lips, her kiss, breasts, or sex. The following examples appear in the earlier poems: "her eager body's unimmortal flower," "of whose tremendous hair that blossom stands/ whereof is most desire," "those/ twain perfect roses," "the warm long flower of unchastity" ("Epithalamion": 3–7); "a fragile smile/ which like a flower lieth," "each breast a blossom is," "ladies like flowers made" ("Puella Mea": 14–21); "thy forehead is a flight of flowers" (III: 25); the "slow/ supple/ flower/ of thy beauty" (V: 27); "her/ mouth the new/ flower" (IV: 34). Conversely, flowers are ladies: "and what were roses. Perfume? . . ./ are they not ladies, ladies of my dreams" (VII: 155). There is in this poem an associational cluster of twilight, dreams, and "nothing," along with the central analogy of flowers as desirable ladies.

The bird is a traditional symbol of joy, aspiration, and of the poet's song, and for Cummings a bird is frequently associated with his lady's eyes—" (while/ within the eyes is dimly heard/ a wistful and precarious bird)" ("Puella Mea": 17). He often pictures birds as flying across a twilight sky, alive with mystery (46: 307; 63: 322; 29: 445), and they are of course associated with the coming of spring, the blossoming of flowers, the budding of trees, and with love (XLIII: 415; XLIX: 419; LI: 420–21; LIV: 422–23; 67: 465; 68: 465–66). But most significantly the bird is for Cummings a symbol of life's truth:

> until and i heard
> a certain a bird
> i dreamed i could sing
> but like nothing
>   are the joys
> of his voice   (XLVII: 418)

Again we may note the association of "dream," "nothing," and "alive" with this symbol.

Mountains dance in the spring (67: 465); they grow and are "so am and i and who" (28: 444); they are the hearts and souls of artists (XX: 401; 19: 439); a true man will "carve immortal jungles of despair/ to hold a mountain's heartbeat in his hand" (XXII: 402); and they are the symbol of a joyful acceptance and a true natural harmony which is fixed and immovable, firm and courageous. Notice, for example, "('fire stop thief help murder save the world'" (XV: 397), in which the contrast is of human alarmism, fear, and do-goodism, as opposed to the mountain's state of spontaneous harmony with the ebb and flow of nature's cycle, and the maples dying in the winter while the pines remain green and alive. And here "nothing," "if," "un," and "snow" are characteristic of Cummings' language and symbolism.

Rain is soft and turns the unworld into the dream world (55: 458); it strikes "realness into form" and creates "blind full steep love" (39: 302); it is feared by men but not by children (XLVII: 256–57); and it resembles his lady (XII: 122–23). Snow similarly transforms, as in "blossoming are people" (32: 446), in which people, the denizens of the unworld, blossom in the snow, "which's" become "who's," "everyone" becomes "noone," flowers are no longer asked after, and lovers are united—this is the "secret" and the "dream" of the poet's imaginative world.

Trees and the ocean find their natural place in such a world:

(Wholly consider how

these immaculate thin
things half daemon half
tree among sunset dream
acute from root to leaf)   (LIII: 261)

Trees grow, blossom, die, and grow again—"so world is a leaf so tree
is a bough" (LIV: 423)—and the sea ebbs and flows to the pull of the
moon, as in "here is the ocean,this is moonlight:say" (LXX: 271) where
the speaker represents himself and his heart as the sea, and his lady as
the moon, the point being that, although the moon can be seen chiefly
at night, his heart keeps following her influence even during the day
when she is generally invisible.

We also get from the above poem some idea of how Cummings uses
the moon as a symbol, but there is much more to it:

luminous tendril of celestial wish

(whying diminutive bright deathlessness
to these my not themselves believing eyes
adventuring,enormous nowhere from)

querying affirmation;virginal

immediacy of precision:more
and perfectly more most ethereal
silence through twilight's mystery made flesh—

dreamslender exquisite white firstful flame

—new moon!as(by the miracle of your
sweet innocence refuted)clumsy some
dull cowardice called a world vanishes,

teach disappearing also me the keen
illimitable secret of begin   (71: 468)

We are prepared by now to recognize the force of such terms and expressions as "whying," "deathlessness," "nowhere," "querying affirmation," "mystery," "dream," "miracle," and "secret of begin," as well as

to understand why the "clumsy some/ dull cowardice called a world vanishes."

Here we notice that the new moon appears during twilight, thus making visible the mystery thereof; twilight and sunset are, indeed, Cummings' focal symbols, for they provide the surrounding setting and background of the others, as for example in "this(let's remember)day died again and" (1: 429), where the symbolic cluster of sunset-twilight-flower-moon, and such conceptual expressions as "dream," "soul immemorially forevering am," "doom" *vs.* "eternity," "soon," "never," and "nowhere," serve as the means by which Cummings creates his poetic universe.

And its season is, of course, spring. Not that Cummings simply is uninterested in the other seasons, for, as we have seen, winter and snow have real significance for him, and so does autumn and, to a lesser extent, summer; but spring, for obvious reasons, means the most to him:

> "sweet spring is your
> time is my time is our
> time for springtime is lovetime
> and viva sweet love"
>
> (LI: 420)

It is characteristic of Cummings that he could never say, as does Eliot, that April is the cruelest month.

Allegory, or personified abstractions in action, is another mark of his mature style. It appears now and then in his early work: "suppose/ Life is an old man carrying flowers on his head./ young death sits in a café/ smiling" (XII: 83); "i am may the first crumb said/ . . . /and number two took up the song,/ might i'm called and did no wrong" (X: 95); "let's take the train/ for because dear/ whispered again/ in never's ear" (VIII: 228); "death(having lost)put on his universe/ and yawned . . ./ Love(having found)wound up such pretty toys" (66: 324). Allegory carries more weight, however, in Cummings' later work—"enters give/ whose lost is his found/ leading love/ whose heart is her mind)" (45: 382); "Soul was(i understand)/ seduced by Life" (23: 442); " 'it's no good pretending/ befriending means loving'/ (sighs mind:and he's clever)" (27: 443). Most of these later allegories deal with Cummings' vocabulary of ideas, involving a grammatical shift as well as a subsequent personification, which argues again for the seriousness of his concern with moral values. And did he not write *Santa Claus* (1945), a morality play in the medieval manner?

Another device of language that is an even more characteristic mark of Cummings' style is the oxymoron or paradox. He used it with much greater frequency in his first volume than ever again, and it seems there a sign of youthful exuberance resulting in a kind of ambiguity which is puzzling to evaluate. What are we to say about "the noise of petals falling silently," "peaceful terrors," "evident invisibles," "large minute hips," "precise clumsy," "grim ecstasy," "the dusty newness of her obsolete gaze," "obscure and obvious hands," or "obscene shy breasts"? It was his early habit to accumulate strings of adjectives, and in many cases mutually contradictory ones, as in "a sodden fastidious normal explosion," as well as synaesthetic ones at the same time, as in "a square murmur, a winsome flatulence." One gets a sense of verbal excess, of a sometimes arbitrary creative flamboyance.

Or is such a device perhaps one more way of insuring conceptual accuracy; does it anticipate his later mysticism, forecast his mature philosophical style? He said, "i am conjugated by the sensual mysticism of entire vertical being" (IX: 150), and such contradictions or attempts at reconciling opposites might symptomatize his early efforts at transcending the discreteness of factual existence, the life of the unworld, without at the same time losing contact with the life of the senses which is clearly of the utmost importance to him.

On the other hand, not only does his use of paradox become less frequent in his later volumes, but it also becomes more functional aesthetically and conceptually. When he says "beyond all hurt of praise" (35: 299), he is not merely toying with words; when he says "i will breathe such crude/ perfection . . . priming at every pore/ a deathless life with magic until peace/ outthunders silence" (45: 307), he means something quite unambiguous; when he says "(really unreal world, will you perhaps do/ the breathing for me while i am away?)" (XVIII: 400), the irony is clear and distinct; when he says "proudly depths above why's first because/ (faith's last doubt and humbly heights below)" (XXXIV: 409), he means just what he says. If the "sensual mysticism" of his early style is suspect, that of his mature manner is thoroughly effective.

Thus his use of symbol, allegory, and paradox amalgamates the abstract and the concrete without fuss and clatter, creating an effect of lucidity, controlled complexity, vividness, and ease, which is the chief distinction of his later work.

II / We may now inquire into Cummings' uses of rhyme, meter, and stanza. There are in general two kinds of rhythmic units available to the poet who works within the established traditions: the regular, in which variations are made upon the basis of measurable patterns of rhyme and meter; and the irregular, in which the basis of variation— if it exists at all—is measurable in less apparent terms. What Cummings adds is a third possibility altogether, which he has done much to introduce into modern poetry—the combination of regular and irregular units, which I shall call the free verse stanza. This third type, although it uses no rhyme or meter, creates the *visual effect* of a regular stanza in that it is broken up into groups of regularly matching lines:

    a like a
    grey
    rock wanderin

    g
    through
    pasture
    wom

    an creature whom
    than
    earth hers

elf
could
silent more no
be   (56: 458)

This poem is built upon a free verse stanzaic pattern in which the
groups of lines alternate from three lines to four, and from three to four
again. The effect is somewhere between the regular rhythmic units of
meter and rhyme and the irregular units of free verse.

It is basically a question of what principle the poet uses to guide himself in ending a line or group of lines. If he uses a certain abstract pattern, he is bound by that choice throughout; but if he uses merely his
spontaneous sense of pause, speed, and emphasis, he cannot tell in advance (nor can the reader) what pattern will emerge. However, I
suppose that a systematic study of Whitman or Sandburg or D. H.
Lawrence would reveal a subconscious normal, or standard, line length
produced by the poet's breathing-speaking-thinking cycle—Whitman,
for example, is a deep-breather, while Cummings normally writes free
verse in short breaths.

With conventional rhyme and meter the pattern of expectations, once
established, more or less takes care of itself, but with free verse it is a
problem of continuous management. Either way the poet makes arbitrary decisions. In the former case his initial choice, however appropriate to begin with, controls perforce the rhythm throughout; in the
latter, his initial choice, although a negative one, forces the poet to
choose anew just where each line will end. Either way—predetermined
pattern or spontaneous sense—some standard or principle becomes the
ultimate court of appeal, and, although the latter is more difficult to
define, both involve willful choices among alternatives. It is a rare
poem indeed that writes itself. Nor does Cummings' free verse stanza
avoid such willfulness; it is rather that he mitigates this effect by
grouping his lines regularly, and yet he does so without restricting in
advance the lengths and ending sounds of those lines. What he can
accomplish by this device is generally a more tentatively delicate
rhythm than the regular stanza can accomplish, combined with a more

strict and unified balance than the irregular free verse paragraph can achieve.

What he can accomplish particularly is an extremely complicated question. I am not sure that there is any significant general correlation between his (or any other poet's) dramatic situations and subjects, on the one hand, and his use of rhythmic devices, on the other. Each poem has its own special tone and attitude, and hence its own rhythmic problems, and the poet simply has to make up his mind as he goes along whether he will use a regular stanza, a free verse arrangement, or some combination. There are, in addition, causal factors existing outside of the poem—such as the poet's temperament, or the fashions of his age—which complicate the matter even further.

In the poem cited above, for example, which is a description of a New Hampshire country wife, the use of a free verse stanzaic pattern, in addition to giving an effect of amplification plus a concomitant sense of retardation, allows Cummings to break down various key words and thereby to create a series of puns. The spacing of "hers/ elf" emphasizes the femaleness of earth and allows it to be compared to an "elf," thus intensifying the dominant descriptive effect of a mysterious and feminine silence. Furthermore, the opening line, "a like a," creates a hovering or see-saw effect which suggests the lady's motion as she wanders, and the split of "wom/ an" allows for a rhyme with "whom" at the end of the following line as well as for a pun on "an creature" for "a creature."

All this is clearly calculated; for Cummings, as I hope to show in the next chapter, is an extraordinarily painstaking craftsman, sometimes writing as many as one or two hundred versions of a single poem before he is satisfied that it is finished (nor does he ever rewrite it once it has been published). But his procedure is actually too subtle to derive critical categories from it. All we can do is to make a few generalizations. (His grouping of lines, first of all, into free verse stanzas is bound by no concern for the integrity of words, sentence structure, metrical pattern, or rhyme scheme, but is rather dictated by the needs of the individual poem) Therefore, in the second place(his lines can vary in length anywhere from a single letter to an entire phrase, clause, or sentence. And, finally, the patterning of line-groups itself has at least six different basic variations: (1) each group can have an equal number of lines; or (2) they can alternate back and forth, as in the above poem; or (3) each group can have one more or one less line than the preceding, as 1-2-3-4 or 4-3-2-1, or there can be some combination, as 1-2-3-4-3-2-1; or (4) there can be a bracket pattern, as 1-4-4-1, or a partial bracket, as 4-4-4-1 or 1-4-4-4; or (5) there can be an alternating increment, as 1-2-1-3-1-4; or (6) there can be an alternating increment plus a bracket, as 1-2-3-2-4-2-5-1.

The use of the regular stanza is an equally important element of Cummings' technique. In fact, more than half of all his poems use rhyme and meter; and although the regular stanza is outnumbered by the free verse and the free verse stanzaic poems in his early work, after *50 Poems* (1940) the regular stanza increases proportionately in importance. (I must modify these observations by pointing out that many of Cummings' regular stanzas are *spaced* irregularly; but this problem I will take up later.)

As for rhyme schemes, there are not many that Cummings has not tried at least once. His favorite ones are the sonnet and the quatrain, which between them account for well over two-thirds of his rhymed poems, the sonnet occurring more than twice as frequently as the quatrain. There are scattered and infrequent couplets, tercets, five-, eight-, nine-, and ten-line stanzas, with six- and seven-line stanzas appearing rather frequently in his last three volumes. He also has written several ballades, and there are a few irregularly rhymed poems.

His handling of the sonnet calls for special comment. In his earlier sonnets, Cummings varied the standard rhyme schemes beyond recognition, roughed up the meter, broke up the lines spatially, and ignored the standard stanzaic divisions, all in an effort to make them look as unsonnet-like as possible. As a result, they were frequently mistaken for irregular free verse poems, and he was fond of pointing out to people who complained of his typographical "eccentricities" that he often wrote in the sonnet form:

Dick Mid's large bluish face without eyebrows

sits in the kitchen nights and chews a two-bit
cigar
    waiting for the bulls to pull his joint.
Jimmie was a dude. Dark hair and nice hands.

with a little eye that rolled and made its point

Jimmie's sister worked for Dick. And had some rows
over percent. The gang got shot up twice, it
operated in the hundred ands

All the chips would kid Jimmie to give them a kiss
but Jimmie lived regular. stewed three times a week.
and slept twice a week with a big toothless girl
in Yonkers.
        Dick Mid's green large three teeth leak

smoke:remembering, two pink big lips curl . . . .

how Jimmie was framed and got his   (XX: 114–15)

The meter of this sonnet, in which the speaker narrates the situation of
a certain kind of man in a certain state of mind, is extremely irregular.
I can find only four pentameter lines—the second, fifth, seventh, and
eighth; and because of the colloquial tone and rhythm of the narrator's
voice and the consequent clustering of spondees and hovering accents,
the remaining lines vary, in scanning, from four to eight stresses. The
rhyme scheme is correspondingly distorted: *a b c d c a b d e f g f g e.*
Nor do the syntactical or typographical breaks match the stanzaic divisions, such as they are—coming in the middle of stanzas as well as anywhere within the lines themselves.

    One could say that such distortions are appropriate to the speaker's
tone and his subject, as well as point out that most of Cummings' first-
published sonnets are irregularized because of his early fondness for
this sort of subject. But I think also that, underlying artistic considera-
tions of this nature, these devices reflect the buoyancy of his youthful

temperament as well as the general suspicion of regularity among the
poets of his day.

His more mature sonnets are more regular in spacing, meter, rhyming, and dividing; but he has, by way of compensation, taken more and more to coined words and half-rhymes:

> true lovers in each happening of their hearts
> live longer than all which and every who;
> despite what fear denies,what hope asserts,
> what falsest both disprove by proving true
>
> (all doubts,all certainties,as villains strive
> and heroes through the mere mind's poor pretend
> —grim comics of duration:only love
> immortally occurs beyond the mind)
>
> such a forever is love's any now
> and her each here is such an everywhere,
> even more true would truest lovers grow
> if out of midnight dropped more suns than are
>
> (yes;and if time should ask into his was
> all shall,their eyes would never miss a yes)   (XXXVI: 410–11)

The meter of this sonnet, in which the speaker celebrates love and
lovers, is quite regular, containing nothing more distorted than the
standard substitutions and variations. The rhyme scheme is the traditional Shakespearian one: *a b a b c d c d e f e f g g*. The syntactical and
typographical breaks fall evenly into three quatrains and a concluding
couplet, with only the expected variations introduced by a few judiciously placed internal pauses. But notice that all the rhymes, except
"who-true" in lines two and four, are half rhymes; notice also that instead of a vulgar subject treated colloquially we have here a traditionally
poetic subject treated in terms of Cummings' special conceptual vocabulary. The distortions are now not so much a matter of roughing up the
meter and rhyme schemes and of breaking up the stanzaic divisions, as

of grammatical coinage and delicately altered rhyming sounds. We might say that such a shift reflects a changing interest in subject matter as well as a more maturely developed set of moral values.

The increased delicacy in rhyming is found in other metrical patterns also—

> who sharpens every dull
> here comes the only man
> reminding with his bell
> to disappear a sun (26: 443)

This produces a wonderfully pleasing effect in such poems as these in which the speaker is praising and celebrating.

His meters vary from two-stress lines to five- and six-stress lines, but pentameter, due to the large proportion of sonnets (not all of which are pentameter), is by far the most frequent. There are very many mixed and irregular meters, while dimeter, tetrameter, and trimeter, in that order, are relatively minor. Cummings' use of the metrical foot is extremely varied, and, even when regular, tends to be alternated:

> what if a much of a which of a wind
> gives the truth to summer's lie;
> bloodies with dizzying leaves the sun
> and yanks immortal stars awry? (XX: 401)

There are also some poems based upon syllabic count, but these represent a relatively minor type.

The use of irregular free verse in which the lines are broken and spaced according to no abstract pattern is proportionately frequent in his earlier volumes—

> Buffalo Bill's
> defunct
>   who used to
>   ride a watersmooth-silver
>   stallion

and break onetwothreefourfive pigeonsjustlikethat
                                        Jesus
he was a handsome man
                          and what i want to know is
how do you like your blueeyed boy
Mister Death   (VIII: 50)

But the use of irregular free verse diminished almost to nothing from
New Poems (1938) on. There has been a corresponding increase, however, in the use of the free verse stanza as opposed to irregular free verse:

a-

float on some
?
i call twilight you

'll see

an in
-ch
of an if

&

who
is
the

)

more
dream than become
more

am than imagine   (XXXI: 407)

This is a poem of reflection in which the speaker is in the process of
turning the observed moon—which is never mentioned explicitly—into
a symbol of true life and imagination. The free verse spacing is built

upon a scheme of alternation within brackets: 1-3-1-3-1-3-1-3-1. No-tice that Cummings' system allows him to use punctuation symbols in a suggestive manner: "?" as the second syllable of "some[thing]" adds the proper degree of hesitancy, while ")" suggests pictorially the slip of a moon which the speaker is describing. Furthermore, "an in/ -ch/ of an if" reinforces this effect: the moon is too delicate and evanescent to name in actual words. Yet at the same time there is within and around these devices a pulsing regularity caused by the line-arrange-ment pattern, a rhythm that prevents the aesthetic effect from becom-ing altogether too volatile.

III / Cummings' distortion of grammatical and syntactical units is his next most radical device. Almost all of his coinages—and a large portion of his vocabulary consists of words that he has invented—are derived by analogy from already existing words. Rarely, if ever, does he make up a word on the basis of root-creation, which produces coin-ages having no previous analog in the language. And of the words that he has thus adapted, by far the largest portion is formed by derivation in which parts of speech are changed, or new words are created by the addition of affixes to already existing words. He indulges less frequently than some have supposed in conversions, or functional shifts, in which one part of speech is made to serve as another without changing the form of the word. Such coinages constitute, we have seen, an impor-tant but limited segment of his style. Nor does he often create words by compounding, as did Dos Passos, or by blending, as did Joyce.

That special segment of his style characterized by conversion, to be-gin with the most obvious, has been fashioned to bear the weight of Cummings' moral ideas. It functions, therefore, aesthetically and con-ceptually in signalizing an individual set of values seen freshly through the distortions of the grammatical shift. Here the chief device is to con-vert other parts of speech into nouns: *verbs* become nouns, as in "he sharpens is to am/ he sharpens say to sing" (26: 443), "he sang his didn't he danced his did" (29: 370), "A world of made/ is not a world of born" (XIV: 397), "the was/ of shall" (XXVI: 404); *pronouns* become nouns, as in "an it that stinks to please" (IX: 394), "when is now and which is Who" (32: 447), "live longer than all which and every who" (XXXVI: 410); *adverbs* become nouns, as in "turn . . . / nowhere to here, never to beautiful" (51: 456), "are flowers neither why nor how" (32: 447); *adjectives* become nouns, as in "the cult of Same" (54: 314); and *conjunctions* become nouns, as in "and finding only why/ smashed it into because" (XXVI: 404).

Other uses of the functional shift are designed for the sake of an aesthetically rhythmic and rhetorically ambiguous effect. Cummings' most common habit is to put an adverb in the place of an adjective modifying a noun: "the slowly town," "loosely voices," "your suddenly body," "exactly cubes," "your suddenly smile," or "my proudly life." Such practice creates structural ambiguities when these words are read as adverbs, on the basis of their form, and as adjectives, on the basis of their position. In this way, Cummings adds another device to his store for creating that delicately hovering effect which is central to his technique and which we have noticed before on several occasions. Furthermore, adverbs can become nouns, as in "withins" or "newlys"; adjectives can become verbs, as in "to frail," "swifts," or "darks"; adjectives can become nouns, as in "boths" and "neithers"; and nouns can become verbs, as in "truthed."

Although many additional coinages are formed by adding prefixes, especially "un-" or "non-," by far the largest proportion is formed by adding suffixes, as "-ness," "-ly," and others. This is a device that has hitherto been almost totally overlooked by Cummings' interpreters.

As for the famous prefixes, there is a definite shift in their use after *VV* (1931), in that "un-" and "non-," having been used chiefly for their aesthetic effect, as in "unserious," "unclever," "unbold," "unsits," and "uneyes," are now used mainly for their conceptual value, as in "unmind," "undeath," "unexist," "unwishing," "unworld," and "unfools of unbeing." In the first case, such a device allows the poet to produce a slightly more vivid impression by using the positive root plus the negative prefix, instead of the negative root itself—"unbold" instead of "timid," for example—while in the second case, he produces increased conceptual emphasis. For example, "unfools of unbeing" means quite clearly people who are too stereotyped to be eccentric—people who are too dead spiritually to exist at all and who call alive individuals fools. Sometimes, so emphatic have such prefixes become in his poetry, he can simply use one as a noun by itself, as in "each more exactly than the other un" (64: 463).

The largest group of coinages is formed by adding suffixes to already existing words, and the greatest number of these is formed by changing the present participle of a verb into an adverb by the addition of "-ly." No verb is an unlikely prospect for such a metamorphosis, but I am speaking now of those that are not normally so changed. "Laughingly," "winningly," or "surprisingly" are, I suppose, common enough forms in current usage; but what about "sayingly," "thinkingly," "happeningly," "lookingly," "collapsingly," "liftingly," "screamingly," "relaxingly," and Cummings' many other similar coinages? Surely these extend and reinforce the range of meaning that he can achieve. Since he is fond, as he said in the foreword to *is 5,* of that precision that creates movement, and since for him living is a miraculous verb of being, he manages by the use of these participial adverbs to preserve the presentness and happeningness of his modifiers. Here is an effect of vitality, of inventiveness, of flexibility; an effect of language growing, developing, and becoming more precise. As is his habit, Cummings is simply extending present practice, doing familiar things in a new way.

To change an adjective into a noun by the addition of "-ness" has frequently a conceptual effect, as in "a peopleshaped toomany-ness . . . a notalive undead too-nearishness" (40: 380), and "bothness," "muchness," "eachness," "allness," or "almostness." Similarly, to form an adjective by adding "-less" or an adverb by adding "-lessly" to some other part of speech helps to express ideas, as for example "touchless," "whyless," "whenless," "thingless," "hereless," "happenless," "foreverless," or in "howlessly," and "wherelessly."

Further analogues are coined by adding suffixes, as indicated by the examples in the following chart:

Adverbs	Adjectives	Nouns	Verbs
riverly	neverish	roundlyness	laughtering
nowly	howish	deeplyness	manying
songly	somewhereish	softliness	leasting
togetherly	nothingish	thelessness	wisdoming
moonly	nearish	dreamlessnesses	onlying
sunly	thingish	skylessness	
fasterishly	itful		
downwardishly	whichful		
groaningishly	oneful		
wellbeishfully	deathful		
birdfully	usful		
foreverfully	mostful		
dreamfully	growingest		
leastfully	nowest		
	beingest		
	girlest		
	givingest		

As with language in general, Cummings regards the question of word order and syntactical arrangement with a curious eye, especially in his later work. And his distortion of the normal sequence of a sentence goes far beyond mere poetic inversion: "My mind to me a kingdom is" seems perfectly intelligible as an example of a certain poetic style, but the following is not immediately recognizable—except as a sample of the style of E. E. Cummings—

nonsun blob a
cold to
skylessness
sticking fire

my are your
are birds our all

and one gone
away the they

leaf of ghosts some
few creep there
here or on
unearth   (I: 389)

Cummings, who was taught Greek and Latin in high school, writes English as if it were an inflected language, as if his words had case endings, as if the grammatical function of words in our language did not depend upon their position in the standard subject-verb-object sequence of our basic sentence structure. His is a calculated dislocation, far from being random or arbitrary; he has a long memory and can keep the elements of a fairly involved sentence suspended almost indefinitely without losing his firm grasp on its structure. What is required of us is that we reconstruct such a sentence by analyzing and synthesizing its parts into their normal order, and in the process we are made to read and explore its possibilities in a more creative way than is usual when dealing with ordinary syntax.

Such creative reading has various effects. In the above description of autumn we are provided with a syntactical equivalent (for the sake of accuracy and precision) of the physical qualities of the scene, as well as with an aesthetic effect of simultaneity in perceiving the scene as a whole as we reassemble it in our mind's eye. The effect caused in the mind by the word order of "my are your/ are birds our all/ and one gone/ away the they" is analogous to the actual visual effect of birds deserting bare branches and winging away, and of leaves drifting and sliding in their dry descent. And because the reader must relocate for himself the parts of this sentence into their normal syntactical pattern, he must receive these impressions piecemeal and hold them in the balance until he explores their pattern, which is then perceived all at once, the pieces falling together in a flash of recognition: "nonsun blob, a cold to-skylessness-sticking fire; the, my, your, our birds, they are one and all gone away; [and] some few ghosts of leaves creep here or there on unearth." Perhaps there is some question as to the syntactical function of "cold," but even that adds to rather than detracts from the meaning, since "cold" modifies the whole picture. Apart from this ambiguity and the characteristic coinages—"nonsun," "skylessness," and "unearth," which are perfectly logical—there is nothing eccentric except the word order.

The trick is to be able to reassemble the word order and, although I have failed with several poems, it is generally true of Cummings' syntactical distortions that they can easily be reconstructed. Furthermore, a syntactical equivalent may be provided, not merely for the physical qualities of some scene, but also for the conceptual qualities of some idea. This may be done by distributing emphases in meaning through dislocation of the word order, as in "i thank You God for most this amazing/ day" (65: 464); or by creating a punning ambiguity, as in "each more exactly than/ the other un good people stare" (64: 463); or by producing a syntactical effect which imitates the sense, as in "me under a opens/ . . . / hole bigger than/ never to have been" (36: 449); or by reinforcing some general movement from chaos to order, as in

army the gradual of unbeing(fro
on stiffening greenly air and to ghosts go
drift slippery hands tease slim float twitter faces)
only stand with me,love!against these its   (35: 448)

Other effects are more purely rhythmical. Take, for example, the following stanza from a poem glorifying lovers:

some or if where
shall breathe a new
(silverly rare
goldenly so)
moon,she is you   (68: 466)

The same general structural distortion is sustained parallelistically in each of the four stanzas of this poem, and the effect is therefore primarily rhythmical, one of pause and acceleration, of repetition and variation, of melody and stress. And such an effect would be entirely lost if the word order were to be reconstructed: "or if somewhere a new moon, so silverly and goldenly rare, shall breathe, she is you." This is not merely a question of breaking up the meter, as would be the case if we were to change "My mind to me a kingdom is" back into "My mind is a kingdom to me." Cummings' poem is built on a general dimeter line, and "or if somewhere" would have served metrically as well as "some or if where." The effect gained is an appropriately delicate and tentative quality, a hovering rhythm caused by the dislocation of word sequence which makes the reader read the line once forwards and once backwards before getting the idea. Other similar rhythmical effects are beautifully achieved in such refrains as "For love are in you am in i are in we" (66: 465), or "with up so floating many bells down" (29: 370).

IV / The spatial distortion of typographical units, Cummings' most radically experimental device, is the obverse of the free verse stanza, which is based upon what might be called "integrative spacing," in that a regularity of pattern is produced by the grouping and separation of lines on the page. Cummings frequently uses space "disintegratively," in that metrical or free verse lines are broken up irregularly, words are joined and split, and so on. Other typographical distortions are found in the unconventional use of parentheses, capital and lower-case letters, punctuation, and the telescoping of a word or the interlacing of several words.

Two attitudes regarding the function of these devices have so far gained currency: that they have no function and had best be ignored, or that their function is mainly visual in reproducing the physical outlines of recognizable objects. Those holding the second view have the further option of claiming this function is either a help or a hindrance, and here we frequently become entangled in a variety of first assumptions as to whether poetry is primarily for the ear or the eye. If we claim that poetry is or should be written for the ear (or at least the mind's ear), then it necessarily follows that visual devices are mere external gimmicks with no real relevance; if, on the other hand, we hold that poetry is (at least by now) mainly visual, then such devices call for serious attention.

But there is a third possibility: these typographical devices may be visual in nature but nonvisual in function. While it is true that many of them are actually unpronounceable, and are therefore visual in function, as was the case, for example, with "?" and ")" in the twilight-moon poem cited earlier, it is not true that Cummings' visual devices are always primarily visual. Indeed, their functions may be described in terms of those conceptual and aesthetic principles that we have been using all along to help explain any poetic device whether traditional or experimental. While Cummings may be using unusual techniques, they are not necessarily any different in what they accomplish from any other device.

To suggest by means of a visual device the sense of some physical object or action, or the implications of some feeling or idea, because it involves a transference of qualities from one thing to another, is essentially figurative. And this is done, in turn, for the sake of greater clarity and precision regarding the thing spoken of. In the case of physical objects and actions it is quite possible to confuse a device with its function and therefore to assume that Cummings intends to provide literal copies of things in the manner of Herbert or Apollinaire. Perhaps this is what is responsible for the pictorial function theory, but we will search in vain through the verse of Cummings for more than a few typographical arrangements resembling such things as hatchets, altars, wings, hearts, or falling rain. What we find primarily, are visual equivalents that are *analogous* rather than *equal* to things, actions, feelings, or ideas.

Typographical distortion may, in the second place, function to regulate the speed of the reader's comprehension of the words and sentences in a poem, and this is an aesthetic effect. Such regulation usually involves a more radical use of the means of creating suspense than is commonly encountered. Cummings will not only withhold the climax of a speech from view until the reader is prepared to receive its maximum impact, as Shakespeare does in many of his sonnets, but he will also withhold the parts of a sentence or of a word. He will, in addition, manipulate spacing and lettering as if they were stage directions indicating where pauses and emphases should come in the reading, and this is clearly an oral effect. The general effect, then, involves surprise, climax, simultaneity, and immediacy.

And finally, visual devices may be used to create or reinforce rhythmic effects. It will be best to take up each device in turn and to discuss its range of functions in terms of these principles. We will then also be able to survey the developments and changes in Cummings' use of typographical distortions.

His handling of capital and lower-case letters is the most obvious, and is aesthetic in helping to produce or delay pauses and emphases, and figurative in providing visual equivalents of the thing spoken of. In the first place, he rarely begins every line with a capital, nor does he begin every sentence or proper noun with a capital, as has become traditional in English typography since the seventeenth or eighteenth century. In this way he wipes the slate clean, as it were, for the appearance of capitals just where he wants them, and, when they do appear, their effect is maximized. He can therefore omit capitals where we would normally expect them, and thereby increase the effect of the lower-case letter, or he can capitalize words or even parts of words where we would not normally expect them, and thereby increase *their* effect.

In "tWeNtY,f i n g e r s" (XXVI: 182), for example, which describes the appearance of the two pairs of hands of two old ladies sitting in the sunlight, the unconventional capitalizing provides a visual equivalent of the actual physical look of their gnarled fingers moving restlessly on their laps. But it is not pictorial imitation: the outlines of the letters on the page in no way literally resemble the twenty gnarled fingers. It is the alternation of lower case and capitals in the first word, the compressed comma, and the expansion of the second word, that *suggest* the appearance and movement of knobby, restless fingers.

Or again, the use of capitals may provide equivalents for ideas, as is the case in the satirical "resist Them Greediest Paws of careful/ time" (XXX: 186), in that the capitals produce an ironic emphasis and a head-line-like slogan; or in "worshipping Same" (55: 314), where "Same," which contains the only capital letter in the entire poem, is emphasized as a noun and as the subject of the poem.

The use of punctuation marks may be similarly unconventional. A poem may end with no punctuation at all, or with such an indeterminate mark as a comma, and give thereby a tentative and continuing effect. Punctuation marks may occur between the words of a single phrase or clause, and even between the letters of a single word. Cummings is fond of using a graduated series of marks—as in ", ; : : ; ,"—to control the lightness and rapidity, the heaviness and slowness, of the reading, or even, in a figurative way, to give a visual sense of progression and development as an equivalent of the meaning:

plato told

him:he couldn't
believe it(jesus

told him;he
wouldn't believe
it)lao

tsze
certainly told
him,and general
(yes

mam)
sherman;
and even
(believe it
or

not)you
told him:i told
him;we told him
(he didn't believe it,no

sir)it took
a nipponized bit of
the old sixth

avenue
el;in the top of his head:to tell

him   (XIII: 396)

Everything in this poem conspires to reinforce the gathering and sub-
siding crescendo of its denunciation: its nine stanzas are arranged upon
a 1-2-3-4-5-4-3-2-1 pattern, and its nine punctuation marks (apart
from the parentheses) are arranged in a balanced pattern whereby the
first matches the ninth, the second the eighth, and so on, while the fifth
or middle is a full colon acting as the hub or pivot.

A similar function is served by the three progressing marks in the
following poem (already cited in the second chapter), but the reader
will note with some surprise that they are meant to be pronounced as
words in order to complete the meter and rhyme scheme:

when your honest redskin toma
hawked and scalped his victim ,

not to save a world for stalin
was he aiming ;

spare the child and spoil the rod
quoth the palmist .   (45: 453–54)

Perhaps even those few poems that I have conceded as unpronounceable are meant seriously to be pronounced, punctuation and all!

Cummings frequently omits the space that conventionally follows a
mark before the next word begins in order to speed up the pause, as in
"a world is for them,them;whose/ death's to be born" (55: 314). Or he
breaks up a single phrase or clause to slow down the reading as well as
reinforce the meaning:

                    Streets
    glit

e. e. cummings: the art of his poetry

```
ter
a,strut:do;colours;are:m,ove                                    (59: 319)
```

The pattern is balanced here—", : ; ; : ,"—which indicates an aesthetic
harmony in the apparently boomingly chaotic scene being described
(Sunday-morning church bells), and which suggests the motion that
the eye perceives among the colors of street and sunlight in witnessing
this scene. The figurative function is even more clear in "(the;mselve;s
a;nd scr;a;tch-ing lousy full.of.rain/ beggars yaw:nstretchy:awn)"
(57: 318), where the spasmodic scratching and stretching and yawn-
ing of the bums is suggested—not imitated—by the spacing of the
words and the intrusion of the marks, which here also follow a
sequence—"; . :". On the other hand, we see the aesthetic function at
work in "Am the glad deep the living from nowh/ -ere(!firm!)" (64:
323), where an increased emphasis is obviously intended. This practice
is different from that of José Garcia Villa, one of the few other poets who
has practiced unconventional punctuation and who dedicated one of his
books to Cummings (*Have Come, Am Here* [1942]). Villa seems to
attach an almost mystical meaning to commas, and he believes that
using them after every word in a given poem lends a special kind of
halo or intensity to the utterance (see *Volume Two* [1949], pp. 5-6).
This is much more abstract and arbitrary than Cummings has ever
cared to be.

Almost every poem that Cummings has written contains a paren-
thesis, but his use of the device is frequently quite conventional in
merely indicating a lowering of the voice for an interpolated comment:

```
so(unlove disappearing)only your
less than guessed more than beauty begins . . .              (65: 323)
```

Parenthetical brackets are often used to help split or combine words for
various purposes:

```
n(o)w
      the
how
    dis(appeared cleverly)world                          (XXXVIII: 250)
```

Here the effect is at once normally parenthetical, figurative, and aesthetically ambiguous. The "n(o)w" is a way of emphasizing the breathlessness of the moment when something (a thunderstorm) is about to begin; "dis(appeared" emphasizes the bottom-dropping-out quality of a darkened world; while "dis(appeared cleverly)world" creates a pun —one world has disappeared and another is appearing to take its place.

Another common use of parentheses is meant to keep parallel two sentences, one inside and one outside the brackets, which run simultaneously throughout the poem:

go(perpe)go

(tu)to(al
adve

nturin
g p
article

s of s
ini
sterd
exte

ri)go to(ty)the(om
nivorou salways lugbrin
g ingseekfindlosin g
motilities
are)go to

the
ant
(al
ways

alingwaysing)
go to the ant thou go
(inging)

to the

ant,thou ant-

eater   (20: 291)

Here the parenthetical sentence reads, "perpetual adventuring particles
of sinister dexterity, omnivorous always lugbringing seekfindlosing
motilities, are always inging [in motion]," while the sentence outside
the brackets, which is telescoped incrementally, reads, "go to the ant,
thou ant-eater." This produces the effect of pause, build-up, halt, and
recapitulation, which suggests visually the scurrying of the ants (inside the brackets) and the anteater waving his snout and flicking his
tongue in hunting them out. And, since the total effect is not revealed
at all until the poem is read to the end and then gone over, Cummings
intensifies the normal effect of suspense, expectation, and surprise we
get from reading any well-written piece, and thereby creates in our
minds a simultaneous impression of a scene emerging from out of
chaos, which again reinforces the intention of the poem.

    The whole poem hinges upon its allusion to Proverbs 6:6—"Go to
the ant, thou sluggard; consider her ways, and be wise." And this is
part of the joke, a delightful burst of pleasure when we realize, after
struggling through the maze of parentheses, syntactical distortions,
coinages, and fragmented words, that Cummings is satirizing a certain
kind of worldly and prudential wisdom. The ant's activity represents
for Cummings merely busy work rather than a model of industry, and
he who is advised to "go to the ant" is the one creature who can possibly profit from such a visit—the anteater. In thus reducing the proverb
to its simply "realistic" aspects—by refusing to make the metaphorical
transference intended—Cummings deflates the whole implied point
of view.

    If such a poem is obscure, it is so not because of the linguistic and
typographical distortions analyzed above but rather because of its allusiveness. And this seems to me the general cause of whatever difficulty
we may encounter in his work, rather than those experimental devices
that have been commonly cited in explanation. Lyric poems are frequently allusive by their very nature because most of them consist of

a single speech without narration and dialogue. Thus the reader must infer whatever details are needed regarding the nature of the situation in order to understand the utterance: why the speaker talks, what he is talking about, the circumstances, whether or not he is talking to any-one else inside the poem, and the like. This making of inferences is, however, one of the chief pleasures afforded to the reader by the form, and the poet must always handle this problem of intelligibility on a general as-little-information-as-possible-but-just-enough-to-be-under-stood basis.

But it is exactly here that Cummings sometimes makes trouble for the reader:

these(whom;pretends

blue nothing)
are
built of soon carved
of to born of
be

One

:petals
him starrily her
and around
ing swim
snowing

ly upward with Joy,

no
where(no)when
may
breathe
so sky so

.wish   (XLIV: 416)

This poem is organized on a free verse stanzaic pattern of 1–5–1–5–1–5–1, and contains many of Cummings' characteristic distortions of grammar, syntax, and punctuation. However, such things do not make it particularly hard to read: "these, whom blue nothing pretends [i.e., dramatized against blue sky], are built of soon, carved of to be born, are One: petals are snowing upward with Joy starrily, swimmingly, around him and her; nowhere, nowhen may breathe so sky, so wish." This is a celebration of "these"; and "soon," "to be born," "nowhen," "so sky," and "so wish" are perfectly intelligible coinages; nor is the syntax hopelessly ambiguous. I am not particularly confident about some of the details, but the general sense of the utterance is clear. What is not so clear is the subject of the speech itself: what or whom are "these"? One frequently puzzles over such a question until one finds the answer, and then the poem seems ridiculously obvious; but sometimes the answer does not come at all, and then the poem remains blank. And what seems clear to one reader may remain forever dark to another.

It is this allusiveness, extremely elliptical, that lies behind most of whatever obscurity we may find in Cummings. Many of his poems refer to other poems, slogans, popular songs, sayings, ads, expressions, paintings, people, or topical events, and most of the time the reader gets the point with pleasure rather than pains. But sometimes he does not, and this is due very rarely to Cummings' use of technical experiments.

What Cummings does with the sentence, line, clause, and phrase, he can do with the word. The technique of the telescopic build-up illustrated in the outside sentence in the previous poem—"go/ go to/ go to the/ go to the ant/ go to the ant thou/ go to the ant, thou ant-eater"— may also be used with a single word, as in "ccocoucougcoughcoughi/ ng" (2: 352). Here the typography provides a figurative equivalent for the action. In another poem the word "star" is built up throughout in this fashion: "s???", "st??", "sta?", "star" (70: 326). Here the point is that the star is a mystery—bright, big, soft, near, calm, deep, alone, and holy—which can only be realized gradually.

Furthermore, words can be joined by interlacing their syllables into one word, as in "alingwaysing" for "always inging," in the anteater poem, or into a mixed sequence of syllables, as in "con ter fusion ror" for "confusion terror" (48: 454). No new portmanteau words are formed by this method; the syllables of two or more words are simply rearranged and combined so that the reader is forced to disentangle and reconstruct them, much in the same fashion as he had to do regarding syntactical distortion and with much the same effect of simultaneity and/or emphasis. We also have here a figurative effect in which visual and syntactical disarrangement provides an equivalent for the actual meaning of the words. So too with the following example:

```
. . . (th
e moon's .al-down)most whis
per(here)ingc r O

wing;ly:cry.be,gi N s . . .                                    (40: 302)
```

Notice how "al-down)most" reinforces the effect of "almost down" by having the reader see "al-down" and then "most," thus forcing him to go back over the phrase and slow down his reading so that the "moon" actually hovers in his mind between "all down" and "almost down." Notice also how "whis/ per(here)ing" emphasizes the nearness of "here" by intruding it in the midst of "whispering," and reinforces the effect of that word by interrupting it and delaying its completion. (Compare also the supporting role played by capitalization and punctuation in producing these effects.)

And, finally, words can be joined, split, or joined and split, with varying results. Consider the following portions of a poem describing a July moon rising above Paris on a Sunday evening:

```
(1)   . . .—the
      moon
      m
      ov—in
      g
      over(moving)you . . .
```

(2)   o
      ver pinkthisgreen acr)o)greenthatpink)
      acrobata

      mong
(3)   trees climbing on
      A

      pi llarofch airso vertheseu pstareth oseings   (2: 277–78)

In the first phrase, "the moon moving," the word "moving" is split into
four parts and distributed into three lines, with the effect of suggesting
the slow motion of the moon rising, as well as of creating puns—"move
in," and "moon moves over you." The word "over" and its various parts
(in this case "ov," which is also part of "move") are repeated in one
guise or another throughout the poem. In the second phrase, words are
joined (as well as split and interlaced) by way of blending the colors,
as we read about them, that are seen in the moon as it rises through the
sunset or twilight; the parentheses, splitting, and interlacing all help to
continue the repetition of the word "over," the "o" of which is itself a
visual imitation of the moon, as well as to suggest figuratively the sense
of "acrobat." The third phrase, "climbing on a pillar of chairs over these
those upstareing things," both splits and joins words by way of continuing the "acrobat" analogy, in which the moon is seen as balancing
precariously over the heads of the audience watching from below. Because the reader must glance forward and backwards throughout the
line as he reads, a balancing effect is created.

   The use of spacing, which may be considered as a device in itself
although it obviously plays a supporting role along with all of these
other devices, may be integrative, or also disintegrative in that metrical
lines are disrupted or free verse strophes are distributed over the page.
Cummings has said he lives in China where a poet is a painter, and he
is, of course, a painter in the literal sense himself. He has a strongly
developed sense of the look and feel of words on a page, which he often
uses visually as if it were a canvas; but the trouble is that many readers
lack this visual and tactile sense and find his typographical distortions

irritating. Although some of his visual devices do function as visual copies of objects or actions, he does not, as I have been arguing, space whole poems to resemble such objects or actions. He may capitalize all the "O's" in a poem about the moon (1: 277), but the poem itself is spaced into three free verse stanzas of four lines each. Or he may suggest or provide an equivalent for a motion, as in "jerk./ ilyr,ushes," which describes how the silence of a lonely Italian train station is broken by the announcement that a train is arriving; or he may work for a visual effect, as in "U/ pcurv E," which describes hills against the sunset; but he does these things inside of the poem as a whole (II: 199–200). He creates no verbal-visual emblems to resemble physical objects. Each poem sets its own pace, suggesting objects or motions, supporting meanings figuratively, distributing emphases, creating puns, accelerating, and retarding; and each poem remains primarily a whole verbal construct rather than a picture in the literal sense. Take the famous grasshopper poem, for example—

<pre>
            r-p-o-p-h-e-s-s-a-g-r
        who
a)s w(e loo)k
upnowgath
        PPEGORHRASS   (13: 286)
</pre>

The appearance of the poem on the page does not resemble, by any stretch of the imagination, a grasshopper leaping. The important fact to grasp is that the spatial arrangement is not imitative in itself, as is the case in representational painting or drawing in which the lines and colors actually resemble some object; it is rather that the spacing is governed by the disruption and blending of syllables and the pause and emphasis of meaning which produce a figurative equivalent for the subject of the poem, as the reader reads in time. As the reader gropes and fumbles his way along this jumble of syllables and letters, his mind is gradually building up the connections which normally obtain among them—"grasshopper, who, as we look, now upgathering into himself, leaps, arriving to become, rearrangingly, a grasshopper." When the reader has reviewed the entire poem once or twice, he recreates in his mind the very effect of a grasshopper leaping, which Cummings is describing as upgathering, leaping, disintegrating, and rearranging. This effect is partially produced by the fact that the syllables of "grasshopper" are rearranged acrostically four times (including the normal spelling); partially by the distribution of parentheses, punctuation marks, and capitals; and partially by the joining, splitting, and spacing of words.

The over-all intent, then, is not primarily visual at all, but rather figurative and aesthetic: Cummings is regulating, with a view to increased precision and vividness of effect, the manner in which the reader reads. The object is, for example, to loosen up the effect of a metrical line, to suggest the thing or idea spoken of, to alter and reinforce meanings, or to amplify and retard. His is a style of constant emphasis: since he relishes each phrase, word, and letter of a poem, he wants the reader to relish them too, and many of his devices are aimed simply at slowing down the reader's intake of the poem. All of this is in line with what we have previously seen regarding his variety, his flexibility, his precision, and his poet's exuberance in handling not only poetic forms, subjects, and devices, but the language and its typographical components as well. Thus, although many descriptive poems may contain visually imitative elements, the effect of suggestion as a whole is produced mainly in the reader's mind as he reads rather than in his eye as he sees.

With regard to the development of Cummings' use of these devices, there are, generally speaking, two periods: up to 1931 or 1935 there is an increase in their use, *No Thanks* (1935) marking the high point in that it contains almost twice as many typographical distortions as any other volume; and after *New Poems* (1938) there is a gradual decline, *1 x 1* (1944) marking the lowest point of this second phase. Several exceptions are found in the use of parentheses and word-joining and -splitting, which seem to persist steadily throughout. The interlacing and telescoping of words seem largely to be confined to the middle decade of 1930–1940 in *VV* (1931), *No Thanks* (1935), *New Poems* (1938), and *50 Poems* (1940). These devices appear rarely in *1 x 1* (1944) and *Xaipe* (1950).

(Can we not say, then, that here as elsewhere Cummings has developed a gradually increasing control over his techniques? Having first discovered what could be done with figurative language, rhyme and meter, grammatical and syntactical distortion, and typography, and then having pushed them to their limits by way of experiment, he is now in the process of consolidating his gains and retrenching his position. We find the same Cummings in the later poems as we do in the earlier, except that it is an older, wiser, and more proficient Cummings. People who have hoped he would abandon his experiments and write like other poets have been repeatedly disappointed at the appearance of each successive volume, and so he has been called a perennial adolescent. It is just not true that he has not developed; but it is a simple rather than a complex development. We cannot have our critical cake and eat it too: some of his most mature and appealing poems are the result of a long life of artistic experiment, and we cannot have one without the other. All good poets are experimental, but Cummings is an experimentalist even among poets. And we owe him our gratitude not only for having taken so many risks but also for having landed safely so many times.)

In the whole composition there should be no word written, of which the tendency, direct or indirect, is not to one pre-established design. And by such means, with such care and skill, a picture is at length painted which leaves in the mind of him who contemplates it with a kindred art, a sense of the fullest satisfaction.

—E. A. Poe, *Hawthorne's "Tales"*

CHAPTER FIVE # creation

Cummings is, then, a poetic maker. This claim is based upon an assumption that a man, to write great poems, needs, in addition to a great moral vision and a flair for language, certain constructive and critical powers pertaining to the organization of a poem—to the adjustment of its various parts and devices to the whole for the sake of achieving a unified effect. It is my purpose in this chapter to demonstrate Cummings' constructive and critical powers in operation.

The above assumption involves, as a corollary, a further notion as to the nature of the compositional process itself. Briefly, it holds that the finished poem is the end product of a series of artistic choices. Somewhere along the line, either as part of his original *donnée* or as an outgrowth of it, the poet develops a conception of the whole, and from then on he works toward that conception, including certain things, altering other things, and rejecting still others, in an effort to embody it most effectively. That is to say, since he must make decisions in the light of some governing conception or principle of organization, his artistic problem is to actualize that conception, from among the alternative possibilities, as vividly and as clearly as possible. He may change this conception as he progresses, he may falter, or he may backtrack, but the finished poem, if it is to be a completed whole, must realize by definition *some* unifying conception as its very reason for being.

And it is this conception that the critic must recover before he can discuss the poem as an artistic whole, for if it was this principle that guided the poet as he wrote, it is just as surely this principle that must guide the critic as he analyzes. How else can he interpret the appropriateness of this or that part, in relation to this or that whole, unless he has first defined the whole? The critical process begins, then, at the end of the artistic process and works backwards, by a series of more or less suitable inferences, from a study of the parts and devices to the formation of an adequate hypothesis as to what is holding them together and giving them direction. Analysis and interpretation are then followed by the process of evaluation regarding the appropriateness of these artistic choices. If that is what he was trying to do, the argument runs, then this is why he must have put certain things here and other things there. And, finally, the argument asks: does this seem the best way of doing it?

This unifying conception may vary from poem to poem, or it may be similar yet embodied in different materials, and the critic had better guide his "series of more or less suitable inferences" by a nice attention to the evidence and all its details. He had better, that is, be as sure as he can that his theory of the whole fits the poem more adequately than the other plausible alternatives. Normally he finds his evidence chiefly within the poem itself; whatever else he can garner from a study of such things as the poet's life, his reading habits, notebooks, prose statements, or traditions, may legitimately serve only as confirmation and support. No amount of research can make a partial poem whole or a bad one good. On this basis, then, the critic attempts his hypothesis.

If, however, one can examine the manuscript variants of a finished poem, then one has that much more internal evidence to go on. In the finished version one sees only what the poet saw fit to retain, in all its complex and unified harmonies; but in the preliminary versions one can see what he saw fit to alter, add, and reject, in all its discordant variations. Thus one's theories as to the poet's artistic choices and their appropriateness may carry more weight. If the composition of a poem involves the solution of an artistic problem, then an examination of its preliminary versions reveals not only the solution found, but also the very process of finding it.

However, since we have manuscript variants for so few poems, their use in support of critical interpretation is limited. A broader reason for making such a study is to reveal something about the artistic powers and habits of a particular poet as well as about the nature of creative, and hence of critical, processes in general, which we can add to our store of knowledge about the poet and the art. And either way, the benefits are many.

I consider myself fortunate in the extreme to have been granted permission by Cummings to study the sheaf of worksheets for "rosetree, rosetree," which his wife had managed to rescue from oblivion. This poem ultimately appeared as #90 in 95 *Poems*.

I / It is time now, in order to prepare the ground for what is to follow, to examine in some detail the completed version of the poem in question as it was actually published:

rosetree,rosetree
—you're a song to see:whose
all(you're a sight to sing)

poems are opening,
as if an earth was
playing at birthdays

each(a wish no
bigger than)in roguish
am of fragrance
dances a honeydunce;
whirling's a frantic
struts a pedantic

proud or humble,
equally they're welcome
—as if the humble proud
youngest bud testified
"giving(and giving
only)is living"

worlds of prose mind
utterly beyond is
brief that how infinite
(deeply immediate
fleet and profound this)
beautiful kindness

sweet such(past can's
every can't)immensest
mysteries contradict
a deathful realm of fact
—by their precision
evolving vision

dreamtree,truthtree
tree of jubilee:with
aeons of(trivial
merely)existence,all
when may not measure
a now of your treasure

blithe each shameless
gaiety of blossom
—blissfully nonchalant
wise and each ignorant
gladness—unteaches
what despair preaches

myriad wonder
people of a person;
joyful your any new
(every more only you)
most emanation
creates creation

lovetree!least the
rose alive must three,must
four and(to quite become
nothing)five times, proclaim
fate isn't fatal
—a heart her each petal

The governing principle of this poem seems to be to represent the
persona as exulting at the sight of bees whirling around a rosetree and
reflecting upon the causes of his exultation, with the end in view of
stimulating in the reader a sympathetic excitement, wonder, and satisfaction as he watches the speaker go through his experience. This is
surely a typically Cummingsesque situation, and it is expressed in his
characteristic manner, which is lucid, melodious, and orderly. But the
truly amazing thing which we will learn upon analyzing the processes
that led up to this final version is how much hard work went into
producing this typical Cummings poem, so sweetly arranged, so wholly
neat. And this in itself is no small gain, for Cummings has been accused throughout his career of lacking in artistic seriousness; and if we
discover nothing else from this study it will suffice if we come away
with an increased respect for the poet's fastidious sense of poetic discipline, which indeed falls just short of obsessive perfectionism.

As a consequence of the attempt to embody the governing principle of the poem in such a way as to make it both intelligible and moving to the reader, Cummings was confronted with at least five interrelated artistic problems: (1) to set the scene so as to provoke in the speaker a feeling of exhilaration at the sight of the rosetree blossoming and the bees whirling about; (2) to present the speaker, accordingly, trying to discover the causes of his emotion and reflecting upon his experience; (3) to work out the symbolic parallels between the scene and the speaker's reflections upon it; (4) to arrange these reflections according to some sequence and in terms of certain elaborations; and (5) to achieve the proper force and clarity of style.

The first problem was solved by means of personifying the rose and the bee in the first two stanzas: the speaker is made to see the flower not only as a sight but also as a song, and therefore it is beautiful and moving not only as a physical object but also as a celebration which involves singing a ceremonial ode for the earth's birthday (spring); this joyousness is that of a party, celebrated also by the bees dancing.

The second problem was partially solved by having the speaker realize, in stanza 3, that the wonder of this sight consists in the generosity that it proclaims, and, in stanza 8, in the creativity that it displays. In order that his speaker's reactions might carry sufficient weight and credibility for the reader, however, Cummings had next to have his speaker ponder over the reasons why this "beautiful kindness" impresses him as having such value. And this he did in stanzas 4, 5, 6, and 7 by having his speaker realize further that the generosity of the buds in so welcoming the bees transcends mind, fact, time, and despair, and is therefore beyond man's ordinary reach. He had finally, and for the same reasons, to have his speaker realize why the creativity that this scene displays impresses him as so joyful; and this he did in stanza 9 by having the speaker explain that such creativity is eternal and therefore symbolizes everlasting life. When each of the five petals falls as the bloom declines, not present death but future regeneration is proclaimed, since the rose, like nature itself, is perennial—and what is more, the bees will return the favor by assisting the process of fertilization, thereby helping to create new seeds for the next birthday of the world. Why

Cummings had his speaker come to two realizations and subsequent explanations, and why he devoted so many stanzas to each, are questions that will be discussed below.

The third problem was to have this already-personified imagery serve, for the sake of economy of means and coherence of effect, as the basis of the speaker's reflective activity. This was done, as the following chart indicates, by means of raising the imagery to the level of symbolism in having it parallel the topics of the speaker's thought:

Image				
spring	rosetree	roses	petals	bee enters
		opening	fall to	buds opening
		buds,	be reborn	with fragrance:
		blossoms		pollination

Personification				
birthday	song	poems	heart	dunce dances
play		blithe		in roguish am
party		shameless		struts
		nonchalant		whirls
		blissful		
		wise		make a wish
		ignorant		give a present
				am welcomes
				humble proud
				people

Symbol				
				joyful
jubilee	love	gladness	fate isn't	wonder
celebration	truth	*vs.* despair	fatal	creation
	dream			living
	treasure			
	timelessness			kindness
	vs. time			*vs.* worlds of
				prose mind
				sweet mysteries
				vs. deathful
				realm of fact
				vision
				precision

It is this imagery, then, personified in terms of the additional birthday imagery, together with its various parts and accoutrements, that supplies the symbolic embodiment of the idea and its parts.

Not only is the choice of this image as a symbol of this idea wholly characteristic of Cummings' art, but so is his handling of it. While the rose as a symbol of living beauty and joy is thoroughly traditional, the rose as a symbol of transcendent deathlessness is not, for when most poets speak of such a flower in this way they rarely fail to emphasize the bitter knowledge that decay and corruption—symbolized by thorn, canker, or its brief life span—are concealed beneath its sweetness. Compare this poem in these respects with Waller's "Go, Lovely Rose," for example. (Most poets have their poems of doubt and dejection, but not Cummings; the natural cycle, after all, both rises and falls, and one can focus just as logically, or poetically, on the rise as on the fall, and without ignoring either one.)

Notice also that it appears to be a real rosetree that the poet addresses and speaks of, that it is used simply as a natural symbol existing as an actual object within the poem. This again is a sign of Cummings' artistic habits, for which we can find an illuminating contrast in Yeats's elaborate symbolic uses of the rose image.

Choosing a central image is not enough in itself, however, to solve the problem of making this poem as effective as possible in embodying its form; for, contrary to current critical assumptions, a central image does not "organize" a poem merely by virtue of being "central." The two related problems of order and scale ensue as a consequence of deciding what kind of sequence to follow, and how much elaboration is necessary. Since this is a dramatic poem representing its speaker as engaged in a reflective activity, Cummings chose to arrange its over-all sequence according to the natural order of the stimulus—the rosetree and the whirling bees, included in stanzas 1 and 2—followed by the response, or the realizations as to why the speaker felt what he did, included in stanzas 3 to 9. But since there are 7 stanzas devoted to the reflective response itself, and since this response does not follow any natural, logical, or temporal order in itself, Cummings had to find some alternative method of handling the order of these portions of the poem.

The method he hit upon was to proceed in terms of a double alternating contrast: the generosity of natural process (stanzas 1–3); the sterility of man's unworld of mind, fact, time, and despair, which such generosity transcends (stanzas 4–7); the creativity of natural process (stanza 8); and the fatality which such creativity transcends (stanza 9). And this is wholly characteristic of Cummings, for his vision, as we have seen, always works in terms of polarities and transcendence. Thus the poem as a whole falls into four sections:

A. Positive: stimulus and first realization
  1. rosetree-poem-birthday
  2. a honeydunce dances in each am of fragrance
  3. welcome-giving-living
B. Negative: explanation of first realization
  4. kindness is beyond mind
  5. mysteries contradict fact
  6. when may not measure now
  7. gladness unteaches what despair preaches
C. Positive: second realization
  8. joyful emanation creates creation
D. Negative: explanation of second realization
  9. fate is not fatal

(I am using "negative" here and throughout simply to designate those stanzas that deal, in one way or another, with the things that the rosetree transcends.) The qualities of this arrangement may be analyzed in terms of *weight,* or the total number of stanzas devoted to each side of this contrast; *balance,* or the position of each group of stanzas in relation to this contrast; and *emphasis,* or the number included in each group in each position. What Cummings is trying to achieve by means of this device of alternating accumulation and contrast includes clarity, force, intensification, and a sense of developing progression, suspense, and climax.

Regarding weight, there are four stanzas devoted to the positive side of the contrast, and five to the negative side. Although it is improbable that Cummings planned it numerically, it does seem clear that he was striving for an effect of asymmetry, that he was trying to avoid a mechanically equal-sided effect. Why he gave the edge to the negative side involves further questions, but here at least we can say that, since the force of the idea is increased by means of contrast, and since he allotted more space to the contrasting stanzas, this imbalance increases the force of his idea. (Of course, there are limits to this as in other things, and he could not have extended his treatment of this contrast without reducing the whole principle to absurdity. Just far enough and no more is the general principle involved here.)

In the matter of balance, we notice that Cummings has arranged a double alternation, beginning with the purely positive side of his contrast, going to the negative, back to the positive, and concluding with the negative once again. It is double, to begin with, to insure maximum impact by repetition and variation—generosity and creativity are, after all, related insights—as well as to gain maximum interest by twice raising and lowering the reader's expectations of the end—but again within reasonable limits. It progresses from positive to negative, in the second place, for the sake of establishing the speaker's awareness of insight in the beginning and his search for its causes afterwards in their natural, cumulative, and climactic order.

Emphasis is distributed according to a 3-4-1-1 pattern. Thus, the first cycle of the repeated alternation carries almost the whole burden of the poem, with the second cycle forming a tail rhyme, as it were, to the whole: 7-2. In this way the central contrast is built up, amplified, and then snapped shut at the end. The first two sections of the total pattern, in following a 3-4 progression, develop an effect of rising intensity, while the last two, in following a 1-1 progression, produce a conclusive, satisfying effect.

Vividness of expression was the poet's next problem (remember that we are following of necessity an analytical rather than a creative order, for it would be impossible to reconstruct the actual "steps" Cummings went through in making these decisions—we can be sure, for one thing, that many decisions were made simultaneously). Vividness of expression involves such various problems of style as rhythm, grammatical forms, syntactical patterns, and diction. As we have seen, Cummings has developed a variety of styles to choose from when writing any given poem, and he will choose that style, as will any good poet, from among the possible alternatives that will suit the needs of that particular poem. Since this poem represents a man responding to the sight of a rosetree and whirling bees in terms of celebrating the joyful generosity and eternal creativity that they symbolize for him, we can infer chiefly that this poem demands a certain emotional quality, elevation of tone, aptness and clarity, profundity of conceptual expression, balance and economy and felicity of style, musicality of stanzaic and auditory structure, and a sweet and light seriousness of manner. Cummings chose to draw upon his neutral style, and from the side closest to his formal style.

His choice of a stanzaic scheme is characteristic of his mature style in its regularity and tightness. Cummings has shown greater preference for the six-line stanza in his most recent work, but this poem seems to be organized more elaborately than usual. The first two rhymes of every stanza, for example, are double and reversed—"rosetree-seewhose," "wishno-roguish," "humble-welcome"—so that the pattern is *ab ba c c d d*. There are, further, many half rhymes which are equally characteristic of his later manner—"was-days," "-ance-unce," "proud-fied." The meter, again, is based on a double system of loose dimeter stress count and a strict count of syllables rather than of feet; and even this is highly varied and intricate. With four or five exceptions and with allowances made for ambiguous pronunciations, the first line of every stanza contains four syllables; the second, third, and fourth contain six; while the fifth and sixth contain five: 4-6-6-6-5-5. And there is, finally, the semblance of a refrain occurring in the first lines of stanzas 1, 6, and 9, where the speaker apostrophizes the rosetree in various ways: "rosetree, rosetree"; "dreamtree,truthtree"; and "lovetree!" Altogether an incredibly intricate system, remarkable if only for the apparent ease with which Cummings has mastered and concealed it.

This poem contains a half-dozen or so of Cummings' characteristic grammatical coinages: "am" as a noun in the second stanza; "can's" and "can't" as nouns in the fifth; "deathful" as an invented adjectival form in the fifth; and "when" and "now" as nouns in the sixth. As is usual in his later style, the grammatical distortions mainly serve conceptual ends: "am" is his way of indicating aliveness; "past can's/ every can't" is his way of saying "beyond the denial of possibilities"; "deathful" converts "death" or "deathly," by analogy with a formation such as "truthful," to a new form; and "when" refers to the measured time of past and future, while "now" means the eternal and immeasurable present. All of these devices serve to portray the speaker's reflections in a condensed, fresh, and vivid manner.

The syntactical patterns, although fairly typical, are not so distorted as Cummings is capable of making them. There are actually only two radical inversions, in the second and fourth stanzas: the first four lines of the second may be read, "in each roguish am of fragrance [i.e., bud], no bigger than a wish, dances a honeydunce [i.e., a bee]"; and the entire fourth stanza may be read, "that brief how infinite, this deeply immediate, fleet, profound, and beautiful kindness is utterly beyond worlds of prose mind." There are several other minor inversions in the fifth stanza—"such sweet immensest mysteries"; in the eighth—"your any new joyful . . . most emanation"; and in the ninth—"the least rose alive." Aside from this, several stanzas involve parallelism and reversed parallelism of similar syllables, phrases, and clauses—another of Cummings' favorite devices: "you're a song to see—you're a sight to sing," in the first stanza; "dances a honeydunce," and "whirling's a frantic—struts a pedantic," in the second; "proud or humble—as if the humble proud," in the third; "that" and "this" in the fourth; and "blithe each shameless—wise and each ignorant," in the seventh. These patterns are created for the sake of the rhythm, the thought, and the melody of the whole.

Again, in the diction, we find some of Cummings' characteristic usages. Words such as song, sing, poems, opening, earth, birthdays, wish, fragrance, proud, humble, giving, living, brief, infinite, deeply, immediate, fleet, profound, beautiful, sweet, immensest, mysteries, precision, vision, dream, truth, gaiety, blissfully, wise, ignorant, gladness, joyful, nothing, heart, and petal are all Cummingsesque words associated with his particular notions of the transcendent dream world of love and fulfillment; while prose, mind, deathful, fact, trivial, existence, when, measure, despair, and fate all constitute his way of signifying the unworld of time, doubt, fear, and limitation. There are, however, several new and atypical words—roguish, honeydunce, pedantic, testified, blithe, nonchalant, myriad, emanation, and proclaim—which seem to have been called to use largely by the needs of this particular poem, and which give a pleasantly new and fresh air to it in spite of the fact that this is obviously a Cummings poem.

Having thus examined the artistic problems which this poem presented to Cummings, and the final solutions that he hit upon regarding the selection, scale, and order of its parts, and the style of its presentation, let us now examine the stages it went through during the process of composition as Cummings worked toward those final solutions.

II / I must first describe the appearance of the manuscripts and explain my method of using them. They came to me in a package of 175 loose sheets, most of which are standard white 8½″ x 11″ unruled typewriter paper. They are numbered on the lower right corner from 1 to 175, but this marking, apparently placed there by Marion Morehouse, serves merely as a convenience to keep track of the total number of sheets rather than to indicate the order in which they were written. The variants are both typed and handwritten (the latter in both pen and pencil), sometimes on both sides of a page, with the typed versions on the lefthand side of the sheet, usually representing a stage of consolidation, and with the handwritten versions on the right, usually representing intermediary revisions and corrections (see plate). It is worthy

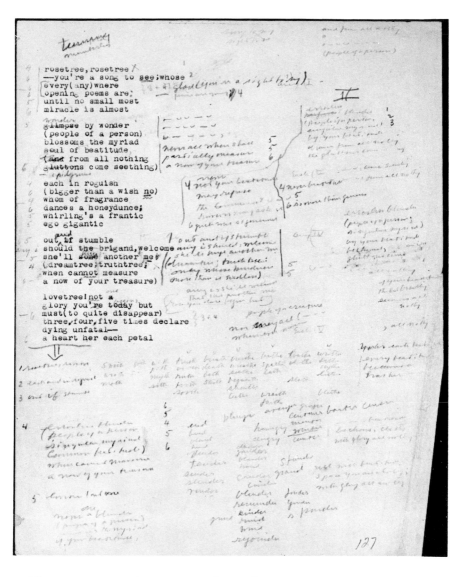

Sheet 127 representing a very early version.
(Solomon E. Wollman, University of Connecticut
photographer.)

of mention that, each time Cummings came to type up a version at some stage of consolidation, he wrote out the whole poem as it then stood. Thus, although there are many handwritten partial versions (sometimes a whole sheet is devoted to variants of a single stanza), there are very many "complete" versions as well. I suppose poets differ in their practice in this matter, some writing out a basic version and then marking all over the same sheet as they revise, others writing out parts separately to be fitted into the basic version during the process; but there is no doubt that Cummings' practice is necessitated by his having to keep the whole poem in front of him during almost every stage of revision.

There are various other markings on the work sheets. These include signs for the meter placed above words and lines or alone in abstract patterns, numbers at the left of lines to indicate syllabic count, signs for the rhyme scheme and lists of rhymes, lines indicating vowel and consonant sound patterns, dots indicating missing lines in order to keep a stanza intact, differently colored pencil marks for underlining, and charts and graphs of various patterns. All of these things, both the quantity of sheets and the variety of markings, serve to indicate visually the extreme care that went into the making of this poem.

The work sheets present a chaotic and discouraging appearance to the analyst, however, and my first problem was to reduce them to manageable proportions. Since the handwritten versions are rather illegible, incomplete, and disorderly, I decided to limit myself mainly to the typed versions, of which there turned out to be 75 sheets—a little more than 40 per cent of the total. Although perhaps a trifle arbitrarily selected from a strictly statistical standpoint, these represent relatively complete versions of one particular stage or another and are wholly legible and orderly, and therefore provide a sound basis from which to make inferences. It must be stressed that I have thus skimmed off the cream from this material and will be able to discuss only a portion of the total evidence available. Even so, this portion was quite difficult to handle.

The second problem was to reconstruct the order in which these 75 sheets were composed. After puzzling over them for some time, I noticed that, although the finished version as well as many manuscript versions contained nine stanzas, many other versions contained less— some five, some six, some seven, and some eight. On this basis I developed the entirely plausible hypothesis that those versions containing five stanzas were written before those containing six, and so on. This hypothesis was later verified by studying the growth of individual stanzas accordingly, for rougher versions were found to occur in stages to which I had assigned early chronological status, and more complete versions were found in stages to which I had assigned a later status. I therefore broke down the process of composition into five chronological stages, and discovered there were 12 variants of the five-stanza version, 3 of the six-stanza version, 41 of the seven-stanza version (the most difficult and crucial stage, apparently), 12 of the eight-stanza version, and 7 of the nine-stanza version.

I also found that the third and fourth stages could be further subdivided in terms of the variations in the sequence of stanzas, assuming that those sequences most closely resembling the final sequence came later than those showing less resemblance to the final form. This assumption was not entirely borne out by further study, however, so I used these subdivisions only as a rough and flexible guide.

Using these chronological breakdowns as a framework within which to work, I discovered that the variants seem to have been called into being by the poet's attempts to solve two main artistic problems: the scale and order of the presentation, involving questions of the number, content, and sequence of stanzas; and the style of the language, involving questions of wording, phrasing, syntax, and the structure of individual stanzas. That is to say, his central intention of representing his persona as reflecting upon the meaning of the emotion that flowers and bees aroused in him, as well as his over-all rhyme and meter pattern, were established, as far as these sheets go, from the outset and remained constant throughout. The variants are concerned mainly with achieving the proper weight, balance, and emphasis regarding the speaker's thoughts, and with attaining the proper felicity of expression within the limits imposed by purpose, idea, image, and rhyme and meter pattern.

Although both problems are worked out simultaneously in the manuscripts, I will separate them for analytical purposes and begin with that of scale and order.

III / Each stanza, in spite of the fact that not one remained exactly the same from stage to stage, does have an essential character and can therefore be roughly identified. For the sake of convenience I will refer to them by number according to their position in the final version. Thus the first five-stanza stage contains stanzas 1, 8, 2, 3, and 9 in that order throughout its twelve versions.

Notice, in the first place, that stanza 8 originally came second and, as it turns out, came second until almost halfway through the entire process. This is entirely appropriate as far as it goes, since stanza 8 is a purely positive stanza and thus belongs with 1, 2, and 3, which are also purely positive stanzas. Otherwise, stanzas 1, 2, and 3 always came together and in that order, while stanza 9 almost always came last. The first stage, then, developed intact what was to be the beginning and ending of the completed poem.

What was missing, of course, involves the entire middle portion, comprising stanzas 4, 5, 6, and 7. We can see that the poem was originally conceived in terms of almost unalloyed celebration, which bears out my earlier hypothesis regarding the completed version, that Cummings felt he could add to the weight and credibility of his speaker's feelings and thoughts by introducing a set of contrasts. It seems wholly natural to have begun in this way. But then the problem became one of introducing and amplifying the central contrasting portion, and consequently of adjusting the over-all balance and emphasis of the poem in terms of what ultimately becomes a double alternating contrast. Since he began with four positive stanzas, it seems entirely logical that, apart from the concluding stanza, he eventually used four negative stanzas, which appear together as a group just off center of the middle of the poem. And these were introduced, as we shall see, in this order—stanzas 6, 4, 7, and 5—through the second, third, fourth, and fifth compositional stages, respectively.

Thus the three versions of the second stage contain stanzas 1, 8, 2, 3, 6, and 9, in that order. Stanza 6 brought in the first of what is to be the central contrasting group by introducing the idea of the timelessness of the present moment ("now") transcending the measure of past and future ("when"). But it was placed next to the concluding negative stanza and after the first four positive stanzas. Cummings now had a better weighting, with 4 positive and 2 negative stanzas; but there is insufficient emphasis, with 4 opposed to 2; and no double contrast.

The third stage, which introduced stanza 4, is the most complex. Stanza 4 brought in the second of what is to be the central contrasting group by introducing the idea of the "beautiful kindness" of the rose-tree (carried on from the giving-living idea being developed in stanza 3) which is beyond "worlds of prose mind." Again, although the problem of weight was steadily being solved—Cummings now had 4 positive and 3 negative stanzas—the problems of balance and emphasis were still open questions, for the 41 versions of this stage vary quite a bit in the placing of stanzas 8, 4, and 6. The first two substages read 1, 8, 2, 3, 6, 4, 9, and 1, 8, 2, 3, 4, 6, 9, respectively. Either way, as we shall see, the idea of alternating contrasts had not yet appeared, for both were arranged in terms of 4 positive stanzas followed by 3 negative stanzas.

It was apparently somewhere in the middle of this third stage that it occurred to Cummings to detach stanza 8 from its positive group and insert it somewhere among the negative group in order to introduce the crucial element of alternation (reading from left to right):

P	N	P	N
1–2–3	6	8	4–9
1–2–3	6–4	8	9
1–2–3	4	8	6–9
1–2–3	4–6	8	9

He now had to choose between the patterns of 3 positive, 1 negative, 1 positive, 2 negative stanzas, or 3 positive, 2 negative, 1 positive, 1 negative stanzas, respectively. Now that the problems of weight and balance were reaching their solutions, the problem of emphasis, of how many stanzas to include in each phase of the alternating contrast, still remained, and Cummings tried in turn several of the many possibilities which were open to him at this time.

In the fourth stage, which introduced stanza 7, the problem of balance was finally solved, that of weight practically solved, while that of emphasis still involved the consideration of a few more alternatives. Stanza 7 brought in the third of the central group with the idea of "gladness [that] unteaches what despair preaches"; and this stanza was placed together with 4 and 6 in various combinations throughout the three or four substages of this main stage. Cummings now had a total of 4 positive stanzas and 4 negative stanzas, and they were arranged in terms of an alternating pattern, the only variation being in the position of 7 within the central group:

P	N	P	N
1-2-3	7-4-6	8	9
1-2-3	4-7-6	8	9
1-2-3	4-6-7	8	9

Finally, in the fifth and last stage, all problems of scale and order—involving questions of weight, balance, and emphasis—were of course resolved. As if he felt the need for offsetting the exact and somewhat mechanical symmetry achieved so far between 4 positive and 4 negative stanzas arranged according to an alternating pattern of 3P-3N-1P-1N, Cummings introduced into the central group, at the culmination of his process of composition, stanza 5, which brought in the idea of sweet mysteries contradicting the deathful realm of fact. Thus he created a cumulative build-up of intensity just before the final and brief concluding contrast ends the poem.

Even though it is by now clear why these groups of stanzas follow one another the way they do, and why each group has a certain number of stanzas, the question still remains, since the variants reveal such differences in their sequence, as to why some stanzas are placed the way they are *within* their groups—namely, the first group of 3 stanzas and the second group of 4 stanzas. We have seen, in the first place, that stanzas 1, 2, and 3, except for the early intrusion of 8, always came together and in that order. Thus it seems that the 3 stanzas of the first group follow a natural stimulus-response sequence: the first begins appropriately with an apostrophe, and introduces the symbolic idea of spring as the earth's birthday, and of the rosetree as a song celebrating the event; the second refers back to the "all poems [buds] are opening" of the first stanza by introducing bees to dance within them, as at a party; while the third continues on to develop the implications of this imagery as the speaker reaches his first stage of insight (is the idea of giving presents at a birthday party somewhere involved here?) in terms of the open generosity of the buds in so welcoming the bees as a symbol of the generosity of life.

With stanzas 4, 5, 6, and 7, however, the order, as we have seen, was fixed only toward the very end of the compositional process and after much variation. This is perhaps because the stanzas must follow a conceptual rather than a natural sequence, and thus their relationships took longer to establish. But as they stand now they follow one another quite appropriately through a particular-general-particular cycle: the fourth stanza develops the importance of the generosity found in the third, in terms of such a kindness being beyond reason; the fifth stanza refers back to this same idea and develops it further in terms of such sweet mysteries (of kindness and generosity) contradicting a sterile, factual view of life, thereby evolving a contrary vision of fertility and imagination; the sixth stanza apostrophizes the rosetree once again in terms of dream and truth being immeasurable by time; and the seventh stanza completes the cycle by returning to each blossom for a second time in terms of gladness transcending despair. Thus, we have been taken from bee and blossom to idea, and back to tree and blossom again. Stanza 8 brings us back to the bees again with "myriad wonder" (recall that this stanza was once second), and stanza 9 concludes fittingly in the only way possible by taking us back to tree, rose, and petal for the last time.

IV / If the solutions to the problems of scale and order involved principles of such complexity, those regarding the problems of grammar, syntax, and diction turn out, upon examination, to have been even more involved.

The first stanza, which was included in all five compositional stages, began with its first, second, and fourth lines almost fixed and was finished sometime during the third stage. One of its earliest versions appeared thus:

> rosetree,rosetree
> —you're a song to see;whose
> high low and everywhere
> opening poems are
> (in each new darling
> is a bee whirling)

What was missing was the effective song-see-sight-sing balance ultimately achieved before this stage was over by the revised third line, "all(you're a sight to sing)." Also missing was the main introductory personified imagery, not achieved until midway through the third stage in lines five and six, of spring as the earth's birthday. "High low and everywhere" is flat and valueless, and so was easily dispensed with, while the bee-whirling image was rejected on the grounds of economy and suggestiveness, because it is duplicated in stanza 2. It was the last two lines that gave Cummings the most trouble:

(1) until no small most   (1a) every small most
    miracle is almost   mystery of almost

(2) so more most than that
    believe we cannot

(3) as if life's kindness   (3a) as if the kindness
    were like death's endless   called beauty were endless

(4) as if our earth has	(4a) lest our earth may
nothing except birthdays	doubt it's her birthday

(4b) until our earth was
really made of birthdays

(4c) until our earth grows
dizzy with birthdays

(4d) as if an earth was
playing at birthdays

(The numbering here and throughout is merely for convenience of reference and, although roughly chronological, does not necessarily indicate compositional stages as described above.) The idea of miracle-mystery, in the first variant, was reserved ultimately for stanza 5; the second is prosaic and almost meaningless; the idea of kindness-beauty, in the third variant, was reserved for stanza 4 to follow up the idea of giving-living in stanza 3; death is an intruder in the opening section of the poem and so was reserved for stanza 5; and the stages of the fourth variant work toward the essential birthday imagery through a gradually more expressive series of verbs, from "has," to "was made," to "may doubt," to "grows dizzy," to "was playing." Clearly, "playing" carries out much better than its alternatives the central imagery of the stanza —song, sing, poems, opening, and birthdays—in that it suits more closely and even augments the idea of a celebration which permeates the entire poem, and which is stated explicitly once again in the word "jubilee" in stanza 6. Then, too, it implies a certain casual fertility on the part of earth, which again ties in with the other related ideas of transcendent generosity and creative emanation developed elsewhere in the poem.

The second stanza, also appearing in all five compositional stages, was similarly almost finished sometime during the third stage, having begun in the first stage with almost all of its main elements in place:

each in roguish
(bigger than a wish no)
whom of fragrance

tumbles a honeydunce
(prances a stumbling
in any trembling)

What was missing here was the final balance of the first two lines, which was achieved sometime during the course of the second and third stages:

each(a wish no
bigger than)in roguish

Also missing was the balance of "dances a honeydunce" in line four. Most of the other variations reveal a search for the proper noun to accompany "of fragrance" in the third line—whom, world, firstful, yes, gift, here, and self were all tried before the final appearance of "am" in the fourth and fifth stages. (Surprisingly enough, Cummings' characteristic conceptual vocabulary still does not come to him automatically!) He was also looking for the proper verb-noun combinations from which to construct the last two lines, "whirling's a frantic" having come sometime during the first stage, while the last line was not fixed until the third stage:

(1) whirling's a hobo   (2) whirling's a frantic
    dances an ego   ego gigantic

(3) whirling's a frantic (4) lewd or pedantic
    joy with gigantic   whirling's a frantic

       (5) whirling's a frantic
           struts a pedantic

There was actually much more variation than is indicated here, but these samples are representative. Most of the variation resulted from an attempt to find the final set of verbs—dances, whirling's, and struts— by experimenting back and forth with half a dozen other alternatives such as tumbles, prances, gambols, and tiptoes. The adjectival nouns in the final version of the last two lines, were at first participles—"prances a stumbling/ in any trembling"—and were probably rejected as adding too much verbal weight even for a stanza that portrays the feverish activity of bees; then the hobo-ego imagery was tried and rejected as a trifle excessive, since "roguish" and "dunce" already bring in more than a suggestion of tramplike eccentricity; "gigantic" is merely a rhyme-word which does not particularly suit the thought; "lewd" was brought in, then rejected as too explicitly sexual; and finally "frantic" and "pedantic" were tried and retained as wholly appropriate to the playing-dancing-celebration imagery because they provide a pleasantly faint echo of the cliché, "trips the light fantastic," and enhance the image of bees stooped bookishly over blossoms, and buzzing from one to the next. In short, this stanza finally achieved with beautiful delicacy the sexual-dance-birthday symbolism of fertility.

The third stanza, which appeared from the beginning, was also practically finished by the third stage. But, unlike the first two stanzas, this one was extremely fluid during the first stage:

(1) out some bungler
   stumble may;the darling
   welcomes another me
   (dreamtree,truthtree:
   only whose kindness
   more than is endless)

(2) out if stumble
   any i should,welcome
   she'll some another me
   (dreamtree;truthtree:
   when cannot measure
   a now of your treasure)

(3) proudest,humblest:
   cannot wait to taste them
   that some another bee
   (dreamtree,truthtree)
   nor gives the zany
   a buzz how many

The apostrophic refrain in line four was finally reserved for stanza 6 in order to achieve that ultimate structural balance of the refrain discussed above, and the kindness-endless idea (cf. the beauty idea already tried in early versions of stanza 1) was reserved for stanza 4 to achieve the sequential amplification also discussed above. The when-measure-now-treasure idea was reserved for stanza 6 for similar reasons. The original versions of this stanza, then, served as the matrix for three separate stanzas of the final version.

Only "welcome" and "proud-humble" were ultimately retained for this stanza—the stumble-bungler-darling-me-taste-zany-buzz alternatives were all rejected as obviously infelicitous. They were probably originally designed to tie in with the rejected lewd-hobo-ego imagery of the early versions of stanza 2 and accordingly were omitted as the latter were omitted. Similarly dizzy-drunken-brigand-clown alternatives were also tried out in the second stage and rejected. We can see that Cummings was attempting to develop the bee-erotic-celebration symbolism already discussed, but at the same time he was trying to keep it within the bounds of artistic suggestiveness. Thus far he was suffering from an embarrassment of riches.

The need for economy was suppressing an exuberant elaboration of this honeydunce imagery and working toward a clarification and development of the speaker's proud-humble-welcome insight. A suggestion of the final version of the last two lines was being worked out somewhere in the first stage:

as if receiving   (or) of living of living
could never equal giving   the secret is giving

Thus, by the second stage all but the third and fourth lines were finished, and the "welcome" idea was extended and deepened accordingly:

proud or humble—
equally they're welcome
free to stay or go
as if the blossom knew
giving,and giving
only,is living

The third line was flat, redundant, and stale, and by the third stage it was revised neatly to balance with the first line—"as if the humble proud." The fourth line was also nearly finished by the third stage: "youngest rose understood," "youngest bud understood," "youngest rose testified," "youngest bud testified." "Blossom" became "bud" to preserve the syllabic count and "knew" became "understood." Possibly "bud" was preferred to "rose" for the sake of variety, and "testified" was preferred to "understood" as projecting the symbolic implications more actively and with less of a tinge of the pathetic fallacy.

Stanza 4, picking up the that-this balance from early versions of stanza 2, and the beauty-kindness idea from early versions of stanzas 1 and 3, did not begin to take shape as an independent stanza until the third compositional stage. It was, in fact, unsettled during the fourth stage, and became fixed only during the fifth:

(1) unlife's prose way
worlds of yea-and-nay choose
only a universe
(who's any rose)prefers
quite such an endless
as beauty is kindness

(2) merely prose dies
foolish any wise,who's
more than all has been and
shall be)rose cannot spend
less than the mindless
(which beauty is)kindness

(3) death his prose mind
roses are beyond;yes
all death would die to have
some(the least)knowledge of
quite such an endless
as beauty is kindness

(4) death his prose mind
poems are beyond;wise
fool,who would die to prove
the nonexistence of
beauty(that kindness
only who's endless)

(5) death his prose mind
utterly beyond is
eager shy foolish that
actual vision;sweet
briefest this endless
beautiful kindness

(6) worlds of prose mind
cannot comprehend this
or that shy eager sweet
here of(immediate
brief and beyondless)
beautiful kindness

(7) worlds of prose mind
utterly beyond is
deep that immediate
briefly how infinite
(fleeting profound this)
beautiful kindness

On the basis of the central prose-worlds-beauty-kindness-mind-prefers-beyond elements, the problem was to follow through with the welcome-giving idea of stanza 3 and to add to or develop the negative elements being transcended. Although this stanza flowed around and about before it achieved the proper phrasing and balance, the idea remained the same; the changes resulted from Cummings' attempts to achieve a greater felicity of style. "Rose" and "poems" became implicit, being referred to by pronouns instead; "dies" and "death" (along with "time" and "lies" not shown in the above variants), which were originally in keeping with earlier versions of the last two lines in stanza 3—"dying's only for the keeping" or "dying's only not to give"—were now reserved for stanza 5 (along with "vision"); the foolish-wise idea was reserved for stanza 7; "more than all has been and/ shall be" blended into stanza 6 and became "aeons of(trivial/ merely)existence" regarding the idea of time expressed as when-now; and the ideas of "unlife's prose way," "yea-and-nay," "knowledge," and "prove" all became embodied more simply and effectively in "worlds of prose mind." (An even earlier version of the opening four lines, not shown above, was "only to grow is/ poetry;and this you/ are(whatsoever doom/ swallows the prose of seem." Cummings evidently began this stanza with certain phrases from his introduction to *Collected Poems* [1938] echoing in his mind, such as "Never the murdered finalities of wherewhen and yesno, . . . only to grow.")

As the final version was approached, the adjectives became a problem: eager-shy-sweet are clearly of less conceptual value than deep-fleet-profound, and their rejection in favor of the second group is another sign of Cummings' gradual development away from some of his youthful excesses to his more mature economies. The remaining problems merely involved the proper placing and balance of words and phrases.

Since the fifth stanza appeared and reached fruition only in the last stage, a description of its growth will cause us much less trouble. Its place was left blank in one version, with six vertical dots to indicate the gap, but then an early draft appeared:

such shy eager
miracles of mercy
forever contradict
a deathful world of fact
by the compassion
of their precision

This stanza apparently absorbed the world-death-vision ideas from early versions of stanza 4 and was thus ultimately conceived as a continuation of that stanza regarding the mysteries of "beautiful kindness" (symbolized in stanza 3 by the buds welcoming the bees) which transcend the realms of prose, reason, and fact (i.e., "death"). The eager-shy-sweet adjectives are rejected carry-overs from stanza 4, but "sweet" is finally used, thus creating a link with the bud-honey-bee imagery but rejecting once again the pathetic fallacy by the omission of "shy" and "eager."

The idea of miracles of mercy and the idea of compassion (cf. miracle-mystery, originally in the earlier versions of stanza 1) were obviously attempts to make an explicit linkage with the idea of "beautiful kindness" in stanza 4, but finally become the implicit "mysteries," to avoid redundancies. Now the mysteries-precision combination suggests a fruitful and appropriate paradox to offset the contradict-fact idea. The final "past can's/ every can't" idea builds up and reinforces the transcendence complex central to stanzas 4, 5, 6, and 7, as did an intermediate version of the final couplet:

by their precision
dooming delusion

This, however, was a bit too negatively expressed for the tone of the whole stanza as it now stands, so it finally became:

—by their precision
evolving vision

The sixth stanza, which became an independent unit in the second stage of composition, took its "dreamtree,truthtree" apostrophic refrain

and its when-measure-now-treasure idea from early versions of stanza 3.
Thus, in amplifying this central contrasting section of his finished version, Cummings used much of the original material that appeared in
his first compositional stage, smoothing out, rearranging, and balancing the whole, thereby achieving and sustaining coherence and unity.
This poem flowered from the seed of a single image-idea complex and
retained its original quality throughout; the miracle is how it grew
from five to nine stanzas, through 175 variants, without losing its in-
tegral character and becoming dissipated by a welter of alien and mis-
directed pressures. Cummings kept his mind consistently on his work
all the way through.

While lines 1, 2, 5, and 6 were fixed in the second stage, lines 3 and
4 remained fluid until the end:

```
dreamtree,truthtree
—tree of jubilee:with
all his(immenser than
everything)nothing,when
shall never measure
a now of your treasure
```

The problem was to find some suitable manner of phrasing lines 3 and
4 to tie in with the idea of "now" transcending "when":

(1) hasbeens of shallbe ten
fold(or ten thousand)when

(2) any(immenser than
every past)future,when

(3) coming all cruel gone
merciless moments,when

(4) aeons of might have been
has been and shall be,when

(5) has beens of shall be till
twilight of doomsday,all
when(etc.)

(6) (neverish trivial
merely existence,all
when(etc.)

The "hasbeens of shallbe" idea, having been rejected from earlier versions of stanza 4, once again failed to find a place. It was no doubt too
clumsy to suit the tone and rhythm of this poem. The other notions
of "immenser," "cruel," "merciless," and "twilight of doomsday," per-

haps having been derived in part as an antithetical continuation of the previous kindness-mercy ideas already discussed, clearly put the wrong emphasis upon the non-transcendental and temporal side of the contrast, for the ultimate modifiers are "trivial" and "merely," which suit the idea much more gracefully. It now remained only to assimilate the balance and the rhythm of the phrasing into the metrical scheme of the stanza as a whole.

Stanza 7, absorbing the wise-foolish idea from earlier versions of the fourth stanza, and the unteaches-preaches idea from earlier versions of the eighth (which, as we have seen, preceded it in the order of composition), came in as an independent unit only in the fourth and fifth stages. In the fourth stage, however, all but the first two lines were fixed:

(1) . . .	(2) . . .
. . .	. . .
happening every	wise your each ignorant
innocent your	(blissfully nonchalant)
glory unteaches	gladness unteaches
more than fear preaches	all despair preaches

Tentative beginnings of lines 1 and 2 involved "whyful answer" and "sermon" (obviously to tie in with "preaches"), but then, since "gladness" opposes "despair" more clearly than "glory," Cummings decided upon "gaiety" as more appropriate to the whole stanza than "answer," which apparently was originally designed to tie in with the teaches-preaches idea. "Shameless-blossom" of the final version is a lovely and appropriate double-reversed rhyme, while "blissfully nonchalant/ wise and each ignorant" ties in effectively with the playing-dances-giving-living *vs.* prose-mind-deathful-fact contrast of the whole in carrying through the celebration of fertile, generous, and paradoxical transcendence over a sterile, selfish, and reasonable fear of life. "Sweet" was once in the place of "blithe," but was ultimately reserved, as we have seen, for stanza 5.

The eighth stanza, which became fixed by the third stage, was

originally second in the earlier stages, and referred then, as now, to a
swarm of bees buzzing in a cluster of rose blossoms as symbolic of
joyful creativity:

(1) glimpse by wonder
    (people of a person)
    blossoms the myriad
    soul of beatitude
    and from all nothing
    gluttons come seething

(2) self by wonder
    (mystery by person)
    miracle by maidenhood
    swarms the beatitude
    nor any,only
    single,glory lonely

(3) wonder by wonder
    (people of a person
    singular myriad)
    grows your beatitude
    till not the small most
    miracle is almost

(4) sans a blunder
    (people of a person)
    blossoms your(soul by glad
    spirit)beatitude
    nor any small most
    miracle is almost

(5) myriad splendor
    (people of a person)
    skilfullest any sweet
    happening your complete
    glory unteaches
    more than fear preaches

(6) myriad wonder
    (people of a person)
    joyfullest every new
    each more completely you
    most emanation
    creates creation

Part of the first and most of the second lines were relatively fixed from
the beginning; the last two lines became fixed in the third stage; while
lines 3 and 4 were more fluid, having become fixed somewhere between stages three and four. "Beatitude," perhaps attempting a pun on
"bee," was a strange word for Cummings to use here, for I know of no
other instance of its use in his poetry. At any rate, it became absorbed
in the developing soul-glory-miracle-spirit idea, which became finally
joyful-new-emanation, a simpler, more economical, and less pretentious
way of putting it. Notice the way in which the sexual implications of
the gluttons-maidenhood imagery, already suggested by the rejected
"lewd" of stanza 2, emerged and became suppressed once again in these
variants—perhaps because the central celebration idea is already suf-

ficiently vivid in the playing-dances-birthday imagery, or perhaps because Cummings was consistently avoiding excessive pathetic fallacies.
What remained was the problem of phrasing melodiously the idea of a
group of individuals ("singular myriad")—blossoms and bees—engaged in a creative interchange of life and joy.

Stanza 9, another of the original first stage, remained relatively fluid
until the end, except for the concluding couplet, which appeared almost
as is from the beginning:

(1) fall if they'll(yes
    this and even this)till
    all disappear to prove
    time's more the fool of love
    than life's fatal—
    a heart is each petal

(2) All and if they'll(yes
    merry one by vestal
    one)vanish into five
    five times their dyings prove
    dying unfatal—
    a heart is each petal

(3) nor one rose you'll
    ever bear but always
    must,to quite disappear
    three four five times declare
    dying unfatal—
    a heart her each petal

(4) lovetree!not one
    blossom you begin but
    shall(to quite disappear)
    three,four,five times declare
    dying unfatal—
    a heart her each petal

(5) lovetree!least the
    wonder you can be must
    (poem or truth or dream)
    five silent times proclaim
    death isn't fatal—
    a heart her each petal

(6) lovetree!least the
    rose alive must three, must
    four and(to disappear
    wholly)five times,declare
    fate isn't fatal
    —a heart her each petal

Since the idea of falling petals symbolizing a renewal of life remained
constant, the problem here was one of phrasing it adequately. The
Shakespearean echo and the vestal idea of the earlier versions were
properly rejected as obviously unsuitable, while the notion of five petals
falling was picked up and developed throughout the stanza as a whole
for the sake of rhythm, balance, and intensity of progression. "All"
was replaced by "least" for the sake of intensification; and "declare,"

which rhymed with "disappear," was then replaced by "proclaim" to rhyme with "become." The phrase "to disappear/ wholly" was replaced by "to quite become/ nothing" as being more forceful, for the implications of being destroyed do more for the idea than did those of being in hiding. Introducing "lovetree!" at the beginning clearly bore out the structure of the apostrophic refrain which was being worked into stanzas 1 and 6. And finally, the balance of "fate isn't fatal" is clearly more melodious than "dying unfatal" or "death isn't fatal" (or "hate alone fatal," "keeping is fatal," and "only fear's fatal," which were other early variants not shown above).

On the whole, then, the movement through the various versions of these several stanzas, regarding the phrasing of imagery, idea, and rhythm, was from flatness, excess, and uncertainty to melody, economy, and control.

To sum up, we have seen that stage three, containing 41 versions, was the crucial one, for, regarding the structure of the whole, the essential notion of double alternation came in during that stage; and regarding the style of the presentation, stanzas 1, 2, 3, 8, and 9 were relatively finished by then (which is only natural, since they were the original stanzas). The last two stages of composition smoothed out the remaining problems of structural weight and emphasis, as well as of the language of stanzas 4, 5, 6, and 7.

What we see, finally, is an intentional artistic process describing a classical three-phase parabola, progressing from stages one and two, through the climactic third, and on to the denouement of the fourth and fifth stages. Thus Cummings solved his basic problem. Since his original conception offered him only a general stimulus-response sequence, the problem was one of the proper alignment of contrasts, and of their phrasing and proportions, in relation to the central insights and reflections of the speaker, which had to be dealt with by sustaining a great fluidity, yet coherence, of stanzaic content and sequence. It is as if his ideas and their alternative modes of representation and expression were circling around the symbol and attaching, splitting off, altering shape, joining and rejoining, moving up and down and around, until finally the whole process, having been kept moving and in the air continuously, somewhere in the third stage began to lock into place and become crystallized. The whole poem was rewritten dozens and dozens of times in its entirety so as to incorporate at each step in the process the new with the old, the altered with the unchanged; it moved forward as a growing and developing unity from stage to stage, adding, changing, rearranging, dropping, and adding bit by bit the elements of the finished design, and "without breaking anything."

I can only hope that I have given some small notion of the way in which the details of this process evolved, and that I have indicated the quality of Cummings' tireless poetic discipline and unfaltering artistic integrity. Even so, there still remains the mystery of how Cummings managed to keep everything going in one direction for so long and with such a miraculous sureness of touch.

We are human beings;for whom birth is a supremely welcome mystery,the mystery of growing:the mystery which happens only and whenever we are faithful to ourselves.

—E. E. Cummings, Introduction to *Collected Poems* (1938)

CONCLUSION growth

Implicit throughout this book is the question of Cummings' development as an artist, and wherever appropriate I have paused to point out changes in his art. It would seem fitting to conclude by summing up these changes in terms of the topics covered by my first four chapters. There are at least two reasons why Cummings' growth has been called into question: first, because many of his critics, being of his generation, have apparently never been able to forget the startling impression that his early work made in their younger days, and therefore

159

have been unable to read his middle and later work without being impressed most by the echoes they find there of the early work; and second, because they cherish a special and limited notion of what constitutes poetic development)

As for the first reason, it seems to me that it is the critics who have remained unchanged and not Cummings. A chronological reading of his complete poetry reveals very real developments in thought, form, expression, and technique, and therefore the facts simply will not support the charge that he has remained static. The critics, in having greeted each new volume in succession with mingled cries of delight and disappointment, either have been unable to read it with open minds or have been looking for a kind of growth that they would not find.

Their view, secondly, of what constitutes development seems to be limited to the kind that involves a reversal of some sort: from profane to sacred verse, as in Donne; from lushness to restraint, as in Yeats; from despair to faith, as in Eliot; or from Marxism to Freudianism to Protestantism, as in Auden. What they require, apparently, is that the poet grow through a series of discarded hopes and repudiated enthusiasms, and this they value as a sign of maturity. This is related also to their doctrine of the tragic vision, of giving the devil his due, on the assumption, it seems, that one can only know in terms of opposites, that Good can be understood only after one has embraced Evil, that the repentant sinner is more to be valued than the consistently virtuous man. Also involved is the rather faddish doctrine that a poet must mirror his times; if the age is complex, then poetry must be complex; if the age is ambivalent, the poet must be ambivalent.

The fact is, however, that many of our best poets have not developed in this way. Did Herbert, or Milton, or Browning? Has Frost, or Pound, or Stevens? If one can grow along a wall like a vine, one can also grow against the weather like a tree; if one poet can develop in terms of reversals, another can develop in terms of a steady progression. Cummings has grown, as we have already seen on several occasions, by remaining faithful to himself; if he has not changed his vision of life, he has nevertheless deepened it and given it a more serious turn;

if he has not evolved from one sort of poetic form to another, he has nevertheless developed a variety of forms and revealed a less purely sensuous emphasis in many of them; if he has shown a consistent preference for certain words, he has nevertheless rejected some and added others in the interest of greater efficiency of style; and if he has not entirely abandoned his more eccentric typographical techniques, he has nevertheless come to use them with less frequency in favor of and in combination with other and stricter disciplines.)

In order to demonstrate the validity of these claims, I shall now examine two poems having the same form, the first chosen from an early period and the second from his later work.

I / Let us examine the first poem:

consider O
woman this
my body.
for it has

lain
with empty arms
upon the giddy hills
to dream of you,

approve these
firm unsated
eyes
which have beheld

night's speechless carnival
the painting
of the dark
with meteors

streaming from playful
immortal hands
the bursting
of the wafted stars

(in time to come you shall
remember of this night amazing
ecstasies   slowly,
in the glutted

heart fleet
flowerterrible
memories
shall

rise, slowly
return upon the
                    red elected lips

scaleless visions)   (I: 31–32)

This is a poem of persuasion representing our persona alone with
his lady at night, and engaged in an effort to convince her of the value
of accepting his love. He argues for this on two grounds: first, that he
comes from having had visions and dreams of her and the glory of
night (stanzas 1–5); and second, that she too, upon remembering this
night in times to come (assuming, I suppose, that she yields), will also
have visions (stanzas 6–8). Clearly, then, his response is given direction by his prior experiences and his knowledge of dreams, as well as
by his character as a detached visionary and a tender lover. We take
pleasure, therefore, in the skill and imaginative quality of his argument as it proceeds, and we take satisfaction in the grounds upon which
it rests: his is a worthy appeal, and his reasons are noble.

There is, however, something of a masculine condescension in his
imperative tone, something just short of self-centered egotism in his
claim that he will be the vehicle of great benefits to her. What is lacking in this situation is any real moral seriousness. His description of
the night as a carnival and of the gods as jugglers does little to elevate
his conception, and his implicit sexual emphases on body, arms, firm,
unsated, playful hands, ecstasies, glutted heart, and red elected lips,
leave that conception just a bit ambiguous. His dreams, and those
"scaleless visions" which he promises her, remain somewhat vague,

referring, if anything, to the beauty of "the giddy hills," the attractions of the lady, the splendors of "night's speechless carnival," and memories of "amazing [sexual?] ecstasies." However it may be, our speaker's visionary powers have apparently not yet transcended the world of physical experience in any real way.

The style is a trifle on the preciously archaic side, including such derivative poeticisms as "consider O/ woman this/ my body," "lain/ with empty arms," "which have beheld," "the wafted stars," and "you shall/ remember of this night." Certain of Cummings' favorite words show up, such as immortal, amazing, heart, memories, dream, bursting, slowly, and visions; but others, such as firm, playful, giddy, ecstasies, and fleet, are the marks more particularly of his early style, gradually dropping out of his vocabulary as he matures.

The use of technical devices is also fairly typical of his early style. Notice, for example, that the poem's imagery turns more upon figures than symbols. One of the most striking elements in its texture is the rather flashy metaphor that makes of the night a carnival, of the streaking meteors a billboard, and of the stars a set of juggler's balls. It is not clear to me, moreover, just how this vision is related, on the one hand, to the dreams of his lady which he has had "upon the giddy hills" and, on the other, to the "scaleless visions" which she will have "in time to come." I think that Cummings hit upon a shiny metaphor, but then let it usurp his control over its place in the development of the whole. The literal imagery does, however, when seen in the total context of his work, aspire to symbolic status—in its association of love, sex, dreams, and visions with hills, night, stars, and flower—but it falls just short because of the lack of conceptual weight in the speaker's arguments. The use of such an oxymoron as "flowerterrible memories" is also a sign of his immaturity, intending as it does to convey general awesomeness rather than anything specifically visionary.

The rhythm of the poem is built upon a typical free verse stanzaic scheme of eight groups of four lines apiece. Regarding grammatical and syntactical experiment, the most significant fact to notice is that there is none, and this is partly due to the lack of any conceptual coinages, which is in turn partly a result of the absence of any real thought in the poem. And regarding typographical distortion, we may note that this is a relatively mild instance of what was to become in his middle period an obsession with spacing. Apart from the lack of standard capitalization, the characteristic use of parentheses, the horizontal space in the sixth stanza which precedes "slowly" for emphasis, and the scattering of the lines of the last stanza, this poem is free of distortion.

I have looked for the weak spots in this poem, or at least for some signs of immaturity, to point up the contrast between this poem and the later one; but I have to confess, since I might be thought to have loaded the dice against this poem, that I have had to look hard in order to find fault. It is a richly worded poem that works surely toward its climax; it is a well-constructed, imaginative, and exciting poem of its kind. However, it is also a youthful poem, a trifle shallow, a bit pretentious, and somewhat vague; and his critics would be justified in complaining of Cummings' immaturity if this were the sort of poem he was still writing today.

II / As proof that it is not, let us examine the second poem.

now all the fingers of this tree(darling)have
hands,and all the hands have people;and
more each particular person is(my love)
alive than every world can understand

and now you are and i am now and we're
a mystery which will never happen again,
a miracle which has never happened before—
and shining this our now must come to then

our then shall be some darkness during which
fingers are without hands;and i have no
you:and all trees are(any more than each
leafless)its silent in forevering snow

—but never fear(my own,my beautiful
my blossoming)for also then's until

(69: 466)

Here, as before, the speaker is represented as being with his lady and attempting to persuade her, but it is apparently spring, and, instead of arguing the value of accepting his embrace, he is engaged in an effort to console her about death. The situation develops in four stages, corresponding to the four stanzas of the poem: first, he comments on the season and the blossoming of the trees; second, he relates the season symbolically to himself and his lady in terms of how alive they are; third, he reminds her of how dead they will be someday (the "season" symbolism being continued in terms of winter); and fourth, he consoles her with his conviction that death does not last. Here again our persona speaks in the character of a detached visionary and a tender lover, with his response being given direction by this character as well as by his conception of life, death, and rebirth expressed in terms of the seasonal cycle. The curve of our emotional responses, therefore, progresses from joy to sorrow, and from there on to a catharsis of these emotions, which is profoundly moving although beyond description.

Where in the first poem there was a slight touch of arrogance, there is here only a perfect humility. This is a serious attempt at consolation that carries real moral conviction, almost strong enough to arouse tears by means of its skillful combination of the speaker's awareness of life and death and love, of the happiness of living and the finality of dying, and of the tenderness with which a man can cherish a woman. Here, if anywhere, is a mature sense of life's realities, and the symbolic contrast between spring and winter is depicted with as full an emphasis upon the one as upon the other. Cummings was thirty years older when he wrote this poem, and so is his speaker. The transcendence is achieved, therefore—and it surely is still being achieved as much in his later as in his earlier work—not out of ignorance but rather out of full knowledge. Our speaker has developed a spiritual power which, in reminding us of such poems as Donne's "Death, Be Not Proud," puts Cummings in the main stream of English visionary poetry.

The style also represents him at the full maturity of his powers, using his own characteristic neutral mode and leaning just a bit toward the formal. Here is his late language of transcendence, including "more each than every," "any more than each," alive, shining, silent, mystery, miracle, and the dialectic of love in "now you are and i am now and we're." There is an intricate system of balanced repetitions and variations in his use of the above phrasing, and of the words "now" and "then," as well as of the terms of endearment addressed to his lady, which are also marks of his later style.

Notice that here the poem's imagery is entirely symbolic in that literal natural phenomena and processes are figuratively interchanged with human phenomena and processes. The speaker's thought turns on this organic relationship rather than on bizarre metaphors. Thus the tree has fingers, its fingers have hands, and its hands have people; similarly, the lovers blossom in the miraculous mystery of spring, their death will be a dark winter in which trees will be bare in the snow, but the lady is still "my blossoming" (In Donne's words, "One short sleep past, we wake eternally,/ And death shall be no more").

In contrast to the free verse stanzas of the first poem, the rhythm in the later poem is patterned along clearly Shakespearean lines, with a regular iambic pentameter and stanzaic divisions forming the three quatrains and couplet of a sonnet. The only variation typifies Cummings' mature manner—there are four pairs of delicately wrought half-rhymes in have-love, we're-before, which-each, and beautiful-until. Similarly, there are the late grammatical and syntactical distortions. The key terms of the speaker's thought are drawn from Cummings' particular conceptual vocabulary: "now" is an adverb made into a noun, and means "life"; "then" is an adverb made into a noun, and means "death"; "until" is a preposition made into an adjective, and means "transitory"; and "its" is a pronoun made into a noun, and means "non-things." Another adverb, "forever," is made into a verb, "to forever," and then into an adjective, by analogy with such forms as falling and pouring, in "forevering snow," which means obviously "an eternal snowfall."

There are three radical inversions of word order which, along with the use of the coined conceptual language, are a sign of the moral seriousness noted above: lines 3 and 4 may be read as "each particular person is more alive than"; line 8 as "this our shining now"; and lines 11–12 as "each more leafless than any." The only marks left of Cummings' middle-period experiments in typography are the lack of standard punctuation, the lack of a space after punctuation marks, and the characteristic use of parentheses.

If these two poems, then, each portraying our persona as persuading his lady, do not establish beyond dispute a real development in Cummings' vision, his handling of a characteristic poetic form, his use of language, and his skill in technique, then no poet has ever developed. For he has grown, as all artists must, by remaining faithful to himself in his own way and by being dedicated as few others are. This is called, all things considered, integrity—which we are prepared by now not to confuse with immaturity—a quality the possession of which by any poet, nay, by any man, qualifies him as a citizen of immortality.

now(more near ourselves than we)
is a bird singing in a tree,
who never sings the same thing twice
and still that singing's always his

—No. 87 of 95 Poems

POSTSCRIPT # 95 poems

What impresses me most about Cummings' latest book of poems, which was published in 1958 after this study was completed, is its vibrant and complex intensity. And this is a remarkable thing, considering that the poet—who has often been deemed a static artist—published it in his sixty-fourth year. I think that this impression of developing intensity has its source in the fact that Cummings has not only deepened and extended his vision but has also perfected several of his devices for expressing that vision. He treats familiar subjects in a continually fresh

way and reaffirms anew an even more transcendental faith in his characteristic acceptance of life and love; he seems to have drained off some
of the public venom from those poems that deal with the underside
of life, and to have introduced a new note of compassionate awareness;
and he is working now a strikingly distinctive vein of paradox.

I / Cummings rarely sings the same thing twice in exactly the way
he sang it before. What is exciting about his new treatment of his cus-
tomary subjects—street and city scenes, country scenes, the seasons, the
weather, the times of day, the heavens and heavenly bodies, birds,
flowers, the sea, and love—is the increasing sharpness of his imagery, an
ever-renewing freshness of language, an unusually provocative and
vivid manner of phrasing, a gradually culminating translucency of
symbolism, and a new pitch of affirmative emotion. It would seem that
Cummings does not return to the same old themes without first having
been moved all over again by the felt pressure of their reality. Such
poems are not simply warmed-over redactions of what he did so much
better when he was younger(A true current of feeling electrifies these
latter-day pages, for Cummings writes only about things that genuinely
move him, and he writes only insofar and as long as they continue to
do so. That is one of the meanings which he attaches to the concept of
growth—to grow is always to be awake to living experience.)
    To cite an example, Cummings has characteristically been fond of
natural settings. But he seems to be developing a special fondness for
what appear to be the environs of his New England summer place.
There is a group of poems in an earlier volume, *Xaipe* (1950), which
apparently have their origin there: #55, which describes the rain over
field and forest; #56, which portrays a heavy farm woman wandering
through a pasture; #58, which depicts a man sharpening a scythe-
blade; #59, which marvels at a newborn horse; and #60, which praises
the boulder, sunlight, and trees of the country. These, however, represent merely an incipient interest which seems to have flowered in the
new volume—so much so that Cummings almost touches upon Robert

Frost's characteristic themes. In 95 *Poems,* consider #21, wherein the speaker reflects upon an abandoned farmhouse being swallowed up by the forest. What Cummings sees, though, is not the moral of Frost's "Directive," but rather the emptiness of all that life which is now gone and which nobody remembers. Or again, consider #86, which describes a black forest pool. What the speaker is prompted to feel is not the relationship between the winter snow and summer foliage of Frost's "Spring Pools," but rather the mysterious impenetrability of the water's surface, which "imagines more than life must die to merely know." (For similar country poems, see numbers 23, 79, 81, 82, 83, and 85.)

Or consider the rain, which the poet observes alone (except for six English sparrows) in the park, in poem #24. He has used this theme before, notably in poem #55 of *Xaipe.* The quality emphasized in the earlier poem is the rain's feathery softness. It is probably a summer rain and the description of its gentleness is enhanced by the supporting typographical devices: the "r's" at the end of "feather" and the beginning of "rain" are joined together to suggest softness; the "o's" of "over," "who," "softer," and "no one" are given prominence to emphasize the speaker's silent wonder. The later work, from 95 *Poems,* depicts an autumn shower and the solitude of the speaker; the quality dwelt upon this time is the heaviness of the downpour, for the poem ends:

```
    . . . t
he rai

n
th
e
raintherain
```

This is getting the most out of a triple repetition rhetorically as well as typographically, for in both ways it suggests the thick falling of the rain—by virtue of its intensity of phrasing as well as its distribution of letter-syllable-word groups. Both poems, then, are built upon a fresh outlook on a similar experience, the later as well as the earlier.

The snow is another image that means as much to Cummings as does the rain: it is the acceptance of the cycles of time and their transitions, not merely the static moments of obvious fruition, which symbolize for him the harmony and the magic of achieving contact with immortality. This is the burden of #4, for example, which ends:

. . . a snowflake twi-
sts
,on
its way to now

-here

A good example of Cummings' continuing use of typographic displacement, this passage also illustrates the increasing functionalism of such a familiar device which is characteristic of this new book. He now more consistently makes words do double duty by splitting them up and thereby creating a charged and punning aura or ghost of ambiguity around the whole poem. The passage just quoted, for instance, clearly creates a montage of "nowhere," or the world of dream and possibility; and the "here and now" turns the latter, therefore, into the former. In #32 of *Xaipe,* on the other hand, Cummings deals with a similar transformation, only he does so explicitly: "all the earth has turned to sky." Similarly, this "turning edge of life," as it is called in #40 of *95 Poems,* turns "sNow" into "Now," in #41, by means of spatial and typographical design.

This device is used again to good effect in the description of a falling leaf—an occurrence which impresses the poet as much as the proverbial fall of the sparrow—which opens the book. Curiously, similar poems also open *50 Poems* (1940) and *1 x 1* (1944). In regard to the poem in the 1940 volume, what impresses the poet is the black silhouette of the bare tree—from which a dropped leaf goes whirling—outlined against the white sky. The typography, as in each of these three poems, stretches the piece vertically down the page to emphasize the falling of the leaf, but beyond this the design creates no extra auras of meaning. In the poem in the 1944 volume, it is the cold, dim sun in the sky, the absence

of birds, and the creeping of the fallen leaves upon the ground that impress the poet. This time, it is more the syntactic disarrangement than
the typography that helps to create the dry, bleak, and discontinuous
bareness of the scene. But in the new volume we are shown the sim-
plest and most effective treatment of all. All that is said is that "a leaf
falls: loneliness"—but it is so spaced as to create a dozen different supporting effects. The first four "lines" consist entirely of one consonant
and one vowel apiece: two "l's," two "f's," three "a's," and one "e." This
pattern suggests, by means of its fluttering alternations, the floating fall
of the leaf:

l(a

le
af
fa

The next "line" consists of a double "ll," thereby suggesting a hovering
pause in its downswing. Then the poem concludes:

s)
one
l

iness

which suggests the hesitant slip and final drop of the leaf. But there is
more, for Cummings gets as much mileage as possible from the word
"loneliness": its spacing brings out at least three more levels of meaning—"alone," "one," and "oneliness." And all of these meanings take
root and blossom as the poem unfolds; they are all precisely suited to
the picture being presented. So, too, did Cummings explore the possibilities of meaning to be found in "nowhere."

If the birds were gone in the autumn of the 1944 volume, Cummings
now recognizes poetically the bluejay and the chickadee who remain
during the bare season to give him courage. The song of a bird frequently provides him with a symbol for the poetry of the dream world.
In poem XLVII of *1 x 1,* for example, he tells how he learned from a
certain bird to feel "how the earth must fly/ if truth is a cry" of a whole

soul, and to sing the "grave gay brave/ bright cry of alive/ with a trill."
But in #87 of the present volume, there "is a bird singing in a tree"
that can reconcile the broken halves of a world and make of a here an
everywhere. That song, apparently, has gained in power in more ways
than one since 1944.

Another one of Cummings' simple but potent symbols is, of course,
the flower—and especially the rose. Thus, in #76, which tells of his
mother's great-grandmother's white rosebush and associates it with
God's heaven, I am reminded of the "heaven of blackred roses" in
which he imagined his departed mother (poem XLIII of *VV* [1931]).
But whereas this early poem was primarily about his parents, and the
roses constituted a lovely supporting image, the later poem is about
God and heaven, and the roses are symbols of Paradise itself. The blossoms of this bush, the poet says, are really dreams of roses; and this
brings us curiously close—for Cummings—to a traditional Christian
symbology:

> "and who" i asked my love "could begin
> to imagine quite such eagerly innocent whoms
> of merciful sweetness except Himself?"
> —"noone
>
> unless it's a smiling" she told me "someone"(and smiled)
>
> "who holds Himself as the little white rose of a child"

The reverent quoting of his lady is very much like that found in #28
of *Xaipe:*

> noone" autumnal this great lady's gaze
>
> enters a sunset "can grow(gracefully or
> otherwise)old. . . .

But in the new poem we have a host of mystical associations. The
speaker asks his lady who could begin to imagine such roses except God
Himself. It could be no one else, she replies, unless it's a smiling someone (the Virgin Mary) who holds God as the little white rose of a
(Christ) child. It is clear here that there are associations established

among roses, God's heaven, dreams, and the imagination. It is not inappropriate, it seems to me, to hear archetypal echoes in this poem of Dante's Beatrice and the paradisal rose. This flower has always epitomized love and spring and rebirth—nor is its traditional religious meaning anything different—and it is in no other sense that Cummings uses it.

The moon is another favorite image which Cummings has been trying repeatedly to capture in the snare of his typographical net, and so we have poems #50 and #51 in *95 Poems*. Compare them with the first poem of *No Thanks* (1935) and poem XXXI of *1 x 1* (1944). In the 1935 poem, Cummings capitalizes all the "o's" in the first two stanzas and all the other letters in the third (and final) stanza. This is apparently a picture of a full moon, and it is shown floating hugely over towns, "slowly sprouting spirit." In the 1944 poem, it appears to be a slim crescent of a moon, but once again it symbolizes the dream world. Here the image is not mentioned specifically, but is rather suggested typographically. Now, in the two new poems, we have the full moon once again, only this time Cummings is concerned not so much with the symbol as with the image itself: with the first poem it is simply the roundness and the seemingly unsupported floatingness of the moon that impress him, and with the second it is the "poor shadoweaten" waning moon at dawn. He can, it seems, look literally and closely, after years, at a physical presence that has long since had symbolic value for him.

Poem #84, however, strikes me as *sui generis*. I do not recall any previous piece devoted exclusively—as is so often the case with star and moon—to the sun and its circuit. According to this poem, whether, goldenly in his fathering, he arrives or departs, the sun brings comfort to his children, for even in his disappearing he leaves a trail of stars in his wake. After discussing the splendors of the sun's coming and going, Cummings postulates a deification of sunrise accompanied by the song of a bird and the destruction of the night's thousand million miracles (the stars). If this should happen, he says, then

—we are himself's own self;his very him

This is an almost religious ecstasy of mystical identification with the father of all life and of all light. For intensity of phrasing, I can recall nothing quite like it in all of Cummings' work.

After the sun sets, however, there still remains the magic of twilight descending amidst the streets of a town, as shown in #48. A deservedly well-known earlier example is "Paris: this April sunset completely utters," which first appeared in *&*. In this youthful poem, the twilight is personified as a lady "carrying in her eyes the dangerous first stars," and the night is personified as a "lithe indolent prostitute" arguing with certain houses. The whole effect is colorful, even gaudy, and deliberately strained in its diction: "bloated rose," "cobalt miles of sky," and "the new moon/ fills abruptly with sudden silver/ these torn pockets of lame and begging colour." But in the mature poem, the speaker, who is wandering the streets at dusk, is almost lifted out of his skin as the visible world of the town disappears with the coming of night and the first star blossoms. It is clearly a moment of mystical transcendence, and, as such, serves to indicate the distance traveled by Cummings' mind and art since 1925.

Similarly, #49 is a poem devoted entirely to that characteristic confrontation of a star by the speaker's soul, and as such recalls the last piece in *No Thanks,* "morsel miraculous and meaningless." In the earlier poem, the poet yearns toward the "isful beckoningly fabulous" star as a symbol of transcendent freedom, while, in the later work, poet and star merge. This is indeed an interesting development, for the earlier poem had concluded with the appeal: "nourish my failure with thy freedom." But in the later poem, the poet and the star, "immeasurable mysteries/ (human one;and one celestial)," although

millionary wherewhens distant,as
reckoned by the unimmortal mind,

. . . . .

. . . stand

soul to soul:freedom to freedom

It would appear, then, that Cummings has made considerable spiritual progress since 1935.

It is from this assured position of transcendence that Cummings by now speaks of love. Perhaps I should say "supertranscendence," for whereas he previously treated love in hyperbolic terms, he now positively outdoes himself in spiritualizing his relationship with his lady. In *1 x 1*, for example, the poet asserts that the wonders of the earth unfold only in his lady's honor (XXXV), and in *Xaipe* he says that nothing may dare be beautiful without these lovers (#68). But consider #88 in *95 Poems,* in which the poet claims that his lady's "fearless and complete love" causes "all safely small/ big wickedly worlds of world [to] disappear." This poem concludes by saying that such a love also causes "words of words/ [to] turn to a silence who's the voice of voice." This is reminiscent of "gesture past fragrance fragrant" (#71 of *No Thanks*), and of "if i sing you are my voice" (#43 of *50 Poems*). These are beautiful lines, but they are transformed infinitely in the line "silence who's the voice of voice," and the only thing to match it is that line already cited—"himself's own self;his very him"—from the new volume. A similar advance in intensity and the use of mystical paradox is found in #12, which concludes by saying that "love is more than love." Even when compared to the great line—"love is the whole and more than all"—which concludes #34 of *50 Poems,* this new one shines advantageously. Consider, again, #94 in the new volume, in which Cummings finds a parallel to lovers in "divinities/ proudly descending," or #71, which concludes:

> . . . we who have wandered down
> from fragrant mountains of eternal now
>
> to frolic in such mysteries as birth
> and death a day(or maybe even less)

This last poem, which depicts the speaker and his lady at the margin of the sea, recalls #41 of *Xaipe.* There the speaker tells his lady that the thundering of the waves upon the shore symbolizes death and chaos and hell, but consoles her with the thought that these waves cannot destroy the imagination. In the later poem, he tells her to imagine that they are as senseless as the "blind sands" upon which the sea leaps and are at the pitiless mercy of "time time time time time." But then he concludes:

—how fortunate are you and i,whose home
is timelessness:we who have wandered down

It would appear that since 1950 the imagination has fulfilled its office.

II / Another change which has occurred during that interval is a softening of Cummings' "dark" poems and a turning therein away from the national scene toward more personal and human concerns. Except for "THANKSGIVING(1956)"—poem #39—which is a bitter protest against our government's official indifference toward the Soviet suppression of the Hungarian revolution, there are no characteristic attacks in this book on mostpeople, bigshots, science, stereotypes, advertising, Fascists, Communists, salesmen, literary fakes, and the like.

What we have instead is a poem such as #30, which presents a slangy examination of the meaning (or meaninglessness) of failure. I am reminded by this poem of XIII in *is 5*, which begins:

it really must
be Nice, never to

have no imagination) . . .

and continues on with a meditation in misery by a fifty-dollar-a-week worker who wonders how it would feel not to be saddled with a wife and child and insomnia. The new poem, however, explains that what got him (whoever he was) was *not* knowing that his whole life was a flop, or even feeling that everything he worked for was less than nothing—these would have been at least something, a sensation of having been in it for a while. What got him was nothing, just plain happening-lessness.

Poem #55 perpetrates a shameless—and, it seems to me, good-natured—pun in attacking the affluent society of the 1950's in America. Nobody wants less, observes the poet, and nobody wants most, because everybody wants more and still more. What the hell *are* we all, he concludes—morticians? This is a long way from the elaborate gusto and venomous sting of "take it from me kiddo," "i sing of Olaf glad and big," "red-rag and pink-flag," and "plato told him," which left such a perceptible mark on his previous work. It may be, since he is learning to incorporate touches of darkness into his affirmative poems, and is managing a more complex art of paradox for doing so, that his well-known scorn (and even petulance) is being drained off from vitriolic satires and being injected into a whole new middle group of poems.

Aside from such things, there is poem #35, which appears to be in a class by itself. A ballad-like dialogue between two country mothers, one looking for her son and the other for her daughter, it hides within its depths such a tangled tale of fornication, incest, murder, and adultery, that it could have been written by a latter-day Thomas Hardy out of one of Faulkner's novels. I do not know quite what to make of this piece, and I do not recall anything like it in all of Cummings' work. These women berate one another like fishwives, and their speech is rendered with wit and skill, but it is not clear just how seriously it all is to be taken. The ending is surely bleak enough, but the whole poem is so outrageously involved and brutal that it might all be a jest.

III / There is, finally, a whole new group of poems which, although basically transcendental, are set vibrating by the conflicting presence of the descendental. Cummings has always been a poet of mystical affirmation, but his insistence upon the reality of the spiritual world has hitherto been accompanied by a denial of the reality of the physical world. Recall, for example, the conclusion of XIV in *1 x 1*:

> . . . —listen:there's a hell
> of a good universe next door;let's go

—or of XVIII in the same volume:

(really unreal world,will you perhaps do
the breathing for me while i am away?)

I have shown how such affirmation has become in *95 Poems* even more
transcendental. What has also happened is that the affirmation is now
frequently accompanied by an acknowledgement of the absolutely real
existence of failure, suffering, time, death, and mortality—even, it turns
out, his own divided nature:

a total stranger one black day
knocked living the hell out of me—

who found forgiveness hard because
my(as it happened)self he was

—but now that fiend and i are such
immortal friends the other's each   (#58)

As far as I can determine, Cummings has never said anything quite like
this before. Consider also in this connection the conclusion to the wonderful poem #10:

For whatever we lose(like a you or a me)
it's always ourselves we find in the sea

It would seem, then, that as a poet of affirmation Cummings is
heightening his art by the poetic recognition, not merely of the presence
of evil in the world, for he has always been concerned with the underside of life, but rather of the impingement of that evil upon the good.
And that is a new note, for they have hitherto been simply opposed as
two mutually exclusive universes—as, for example, in "here is a secret
they never will share" of #66 in *Xaipe*. But now, as in #18 of the new
volume, he affirms that we must all lie as low in the dust as flowers
when their time is past, and that all flesh is "If" and all blood is "When."
In poem #57 he opposes youth and age, and then concludes by noting
how "youth goes right on growing old." And in #94 he can ask, "do
lovers suffer?"

But make no mistake. Cummings is still the poet of transcendence, and no amount of sophistication will ever hinder his soaring flight. What he has done in 95 *Poems,* however, is to incorporate into the structure of his joyful song the very fabric of negation itself. The result is a new sense of what paradox can do. For if the affirmative transcends the negative, then how much more intense will be that affirmation which can transcend the negative even though or because it is in the grips of that very negative. Failure means success, for example, and this hinges upon an apparent contradiction which can be resolved only after the several meanings of these words have been sorted out. This tends to produce, as we all know, a high degree of poetic excitement.

Cummings has dealt on occasion in recent volumes with paradox as a necessary device for expressing the ineffable of the mystic's vision. Recall, for instance, the conclusion of XVI in *1 x 1*—"All lose,whole find," or of XX in the same volume—"the most who die,the more we live." But something more is happening in 95 *Poems;* such a device is becoming not only more frequent but also more inclusive and eloquent. What is being included is an acknowledgement of the reality of the world of appearance:

now air is air and thing is thing:no bliss

of heavenly earth beguiles our spirits,whose
miraculously disenchanted eyes

live the magnificent honesty of space.   (#3)

What has happened in this poem is that summer has gone and winter is on its way.

Whereas opposites had been habitually opposed and similarities habitually paired, it would now appear that they may be—not reconciled, to be sure—but rather incorporated into the same structure by means of an apparent contradiction. Poem #16 provides a breath-takingly beautiful example of this new note. Built upon five stanzaic blocks (tercets), its first four stanzas circle gracefully around the varied restatement of opposites. It is the time of spring, when the world and the imagination come alive, and forgetting why,remember how

    .   .   .   .   .

remember so(forgetting seem)

    .   .   .   .   .

forgetting if,remember yes

    .   .   .   .   .

remember seek(forgetting find)

conclude the stanzas, saying: forget the itch of the brain to seek reasons, and remember to open your eyes to what is happening around you; remember that the imagination is more real than reality, and forget the mere appearance of reality; forget your fears, and remember your hopes; remember that the goal of life is the search itself, and forget about finding stability and certainty. So far this is predictable Cummings, but look what happens in the last stanza:

and in a mystery to be
(when time from time shall set us free)
forgetting me,remember me

The same opposition is prepared for and the alternating sequence of the four preceding stanzas seems about to be completed. But instead of following suit with one more pair of opposed opposites to match the why-how, so-seem, and seek-find dichotomy already built up, Cummings surprisingly snaps the whole poem shut with a startling paradox which is created by playing off against each other not clear-cut opposites but rather the opposing meanings of the same word.

The over-all meaning of the poem is somewhat as follows: *in* time, the poet tells his lady, while we are still a part of the physical world, you should be reminded by the spring to remember the ultimate importance of growth, dream, affirmation, and possibility—which are the material gateways to and symbols of the timeless world—and to forget questions, appearances, doubts, and results—which are the trivial and finite aspects of mere actuality; and *out* of time, when we shall have entered that transcendental world (after death), you should remember the part of my life which, through love, partakes of immortality; and forget that part, the merely material existence, which is mortal and ephemeral. The point is that there is an implied recognition that the speaker is compounded of both parts. Thus the final line seems to me to be brilliantly effective: not only does it surprise (because it was unexpected), but it also makes profound sense after the reader's mind has bridged the gap made by the paradox.

Consider, again, poem #25, which presents the speaker as reflecting on the significance of an organ-grinder and his cockatoo performing along 14th Street. When you ask this melancholy fellow to give you your fortune, he taps with his stick at a cage he is carrying and out steps the cockatoo, who mounts the stick and is carried to an open drawer of the hand organ. The bird tweaks from out of this drawer a faded piece of pitiful paper and, bowing, proffers you the meaning of the stars. The poet is swept away by a gust of sorrow at this sight:

>   . . . Because
> only the truest things always
>
> are true because they can't be true

Similarly, in poem #48, as the speaker watches the world float away at the descent of twilight, he feels that "the departure of everything real is the/ arrival of everything true." In poem #78, he asserts: "Time's strange fellow;/ more he gives than takes/ (and he takes all)." In poem #70, he speculates, in the last stanza, on the relationship of beauty to life and death: life is a "blunder" which "we die to breathe," but if beauty should touch life then it becomes her wonder—

> —and wonderful is death;
> but more,the older he's
> the younger she's

The one thing that has marked the curve of Cummings' development as he has gotten older is the range and depth of his responsiveness

to the approach of death. As the poet becomes aware of the encroach-
ments of age, so too does the speaker of his poems. And in a way, this
is a vindication of all that optimism he has been expressing throughout
his career, for without an answer to death it would all have been useless. How ignoble to speak during one's entire life of the ultimate
reality of the spiritual world and then to collapse in terror before the
final dissolution of the physical. But Cummings speaks of it in poem
#3, already referred to, as "that white sleep wherein all human curi-
osity we'll spend"; and he speaks of "the courage to receive time's
mightiest dream" which that sleep promises to create. And in poem #11
he plays variations on the biblical theme:

> —a time for growing and a time for dying:
> a night for silence and a day for singing
>
> but more than all(as all your more than eyes
> tell me)there is a time for timelessness

No more dignified way of conceiving the end can be imagined; no
more artistic way of climaxing a lifelong poetic career can be conceived.

SUBJECT INDEX

INDEX OF FIRST LINES

voices to voices, lip to lip, 14
weazened Irrefutable unastonished, 113
what does little Ernest croon, 51, 52, 54, 76
what Got him was Noth, 177
what if a much of a which of a wind, 17, 19, 37, 38–39, 93, 103, 180
what time is it i wonder never mind, 58
whatever's merely wilful, 182
when faces called flowers float out of the ground, 92–93
when/ from a sidewalk, 116
when god decided to invent, 20, 106
when rain whom fear, 93
when serpents bargain for the right to squirm, 18
when you are silent,shining host by guest, 22
when your honest redskin toma, 48, 115
which is the very, 72–73
whippoorwill this, 170
who before dying demands not rebirth, 13
who knows if the moon's, 15–16
who sharpens every dull, 89–90, 103, 105
who were so dark of heart they might not speak, 30, 106
whose are these(wraith a clinging with a wraith), 69–70, 176–177
why are these pipples taking their hets off?, 11, 79
workingman with hand so hairy-sturdy, 53, 81
worshipping Same, 13, 114, 115

y is a WELL KNOWN ATHLETE'S BRIDE, 78
yes is a pleasant country, 58–59
ygUDuh, 53, 76
yonder deadfromtheneckup graduate of a, 79
you no, 177–178
yours is the music for no instrument, 11